Foreword

This eight-country investigation into how students can be encouraged to become lifelong learners is the latest publication in the *What Works in Innovation in Education* series produced by the OECD's Centre for Educational Research and Innovation (CERI).

Each year since 1993, CERI has carried out an empirically-based study of an important education issue and pointed to some of the most exciting innovations that are taking place in that field. Previous studies have examined such topics as school choice, career guidance, in-service training of teachers and ways of tackling social exclusion through adult learning.

As with earlier studies, the intention this year is not to produce a technical report or an exhaustive analysis of academic research in this area. The *What Works in Innovation in Education* studies are aimed at a broad OECD-wide audience that includes educational policy-makers, practitioners and parents. They also have a very tight time-schedule – country visits and the resulting reports are generally completed within five months. But the speed with which the operation is carried out ensures that the information and analysis provided are unusually up-to-date.

This year's report focuses on secondary schools and a variety of youth projects. It involved eight countries – Denmark, Finland, Iceland, Ireland, Japan, Korea, Norway and the United Kingdom – and is based on:

- Background reports prepared by experts appointed by each participating country.

- Visits to the eight countries by the OCED Secretariat and/or consultants to the study. They carried out a detailed examination of 24 initiatives – three in each country – that had been identified as particularly effective at raising motivation levels.

- Previous OECD reports and other research literature.

Part I of this report provides a synthesis of the main issues and trends relating to student motivation for lifelong learning. It concludes with a set of *key policy considerations*. Part II consists of eight country chapters that contain background information on national policy approaches as well as descriptions of the innovative work being undertaken in the schools and youth projects visited.

Under the overall responsibility of the CERI Secretariat, David Budge of *The Times Educational Supplement* prepared the report. Within the Secretariat, the responsible official was Motoyo Kamiya, and she also contributed to the drafting. Two other officials, Peter Evans and David Istance, also made significant contributions to the report.

The report is published on the responsibility of the Secretary-General.

Table of Contents

Part II
Country Case Studies

Acknowledgements

We appreciate the work and support of country experts: Mr. Peter Bacher (Denmark), Ms. Marja-Liisa Karpinnen (Finland), Mr. Fjölnir Ásbjörnsson (Iceland), Prof. Áine Hyland (Ireland), Prof. Masahiro Konno (Japan), Ms. Sookyoung Lee (Korea), Ms. Marit Egge (Norway) and Dr. Derrick Armstrong (United Kingdom). We are also grateful for contributions made by consultants: Mr. Olivier Bertrand, Prof. Áine Hyland (Ireland), Mr. John Walsh and Mr. Michael Williams.

This study has been made possible by the financial assistance, through voluntary contributions, of the Ministry of Education of Denmark, the National Board of Education in Finland, the Department of Education and Science of Iceland, the Department of Education and Science of Ireland, The Ministry of Education, Science, Sports and Culture in Japan, the Ministry of Education of Korea, the Ministry of Education and Church Affairs of Norway, and the Department of Education and Employment in the United Kingdom.

Introduction

An age-old conundrum – how to engage and maintain teenagers' interest in school "work" – continues to baffle and frustrate teachers around the world.

Young children rarely lack curiosity, but as they enter the teenage years their appetite for learning often appears to shrink. Many eventually drop out before the end of compulsory schooling. Others continue to turn up for school but make the minimum effort. They are present in body, but not in mind.

Such problems are generally associated with Western countries but even Japan and Korea, two of the most academically successful Pacific Rim nations, are not immune. More than 100 000 Japanese children now truant and only one-third of Korean teenagers are said to be satisfied with high school life.

These statistics would be worrying at any time, but as Chapter 1 of this report explains, they take on new significance in an era when one of the essential survival tools for individuals – and nations – is a willingness to learn and re-learn.

The OECD first acknowledged the importance of lifelong learning to achieve a range of educational, social and economic objectives at least 20 years ago. More recently, a 1996 meeting of OECD education ministers reaffirmed the importance of "lifelong learning for all" and emphasised that this goal could only be achieved if firm foundations were laid in primary and secondary schools.

Member governments have since been working towards this goal but the speed of change makes it imperative that lifelong learning remains at the top of national agendas. As this report reminds us, it is not simply a case of preparing young people for several changes of career. By 2010, many of today's 18-year-olds will be doing jobs that do not even exist at present.

So what can governments and education systems do to inculcate the "zest for learning" that young people will need if they are to thrive in 21st-century post-industrial societies? This was one of the key questions that we have set out to answer in this, the eighth of the *What Works in Innovation* studies produced by the OECD's Centre for Educational Research and Innovation.

We do not pretend to offer magic solutions, but during our visits to the eight countries that participated in this study we encountered many innovative schemes that appear to be developing the skills and attitudes necessary for lifelong learning. The 24 initiatives that Member governments offered as examples of good practice are described in Part II.

Part I begins with an explanation of why trends such as globalisation, trade liberalisation and ageing populations make lifelong learning so crucial. Chapter I also illustrates why the responsibility for motivating children cannot be borne by schools alone. Governments, employers and parents must play their part.

The importance of parents, and indeed national attitudes towards education, is underlined in Chapter 2 which provides a digest of some of the most significant research findings in this field. Motivation is a notoriously complex topic to research because a child's attitude to learning can be affected by an almost infinite number and combination of psychological, physical, educational and social factors. Nevertheless, some of the researchers' insights are extremely useful and deserve to be much more widely disseminated.

Chapter 3 examines the policies that national and local government are adopting in an attempt to raise young people's motivation levels. Two important concepts – individuality and diversity – appear to be underpinning the actions of most countries. The first is associated with student-centred learning, the second with the growing range of educational pathways that are opening up, especially in countries where the traditional barriers between academic and vocational studies are being dismantled.

In Chapter 4 we compare our findings with those of previous research and point to the key policy considerations that this study has highlighted. They include:

- *Assessment*: Some children are stimulated by high-stakes exams; others are crippled by them. Should higher-education institutions and employers therefore be more prepared to accept other forms of accreditation?

- *Teachers*: How can we motivate more teachers to embrace lifelong learning? Unless we do, there is little likelihood that their students will maintain their curiosity into adulthood.

- *More able students*: While it is only proper that so many student-motivation programmes focus on the disadvantaged and disaffected there is a danger of neglecting the needs of students who may be more able but may not be equipped for lifelong learning.

- *Gender*: In some countries more attention could be paid to the different motivation levels of boys and girls in specific subjects – for example, boys' relative disinterest in languages and girls' in maths and science.

It is generally accepted that countries must find their own solutions to such problems because national education systems are highly individualistic. That is undoubtedly true, but the most effective motivation strategies discussed in this book are likely to have trans-national appeal. Policy-makers and others who recognise the importance of creating a new generation of lifelong-learners should therefore find much to interest them in the following chapters.

SYNTHESIS OF THE MAIN ISSUES AND TRENDS

Chapter 1

Why Motivation for Lifelong Learning is so Important

Harvard educationist Robert Kegan has used a motoring analogy to describe the fundamental change that many countries are experiencing at the beginning of the new millennium. Kegan believes that nations have in recent years been moving from an "automatic" to a "stick-shift" culture. In an automatic car, drivers have little control over the changing of gears. Similarly, in a traditional "automatic" society, decisions about who to be and how to earn a living are largely pre-ordained. But in a "stick-shift" society, as in a manual car, the individual assumes greater responsibilities. In this new culture we become individual choosers who must be highly adaptable if we and the society we live in are to thrive (Kegan, 1994).

This interpretation of the world does not take into account the many millions whose life choices are severely constrained by poverty. No less than 20 per cent of children in European Union countries and the United States are living in poor households. Nevertheless, Kegan's thesis is insightful and it helps to explain why the issue addressed in this book – motivating children for lifelong learning – is of such significance to OECD countries.

It can, of course, be argued that the motivation of students for lifelong learning has always been important. Certainly the ability to challenge the unmotivated is one of the hallmarks of a truly professional teacher. But even in the recent past, there was little talk of lifelong learning. There was merely a general hope that young people would maintain an interest in art, music, science and public affairs after leaving school. That remains as vital as it ever was, but today there are also other pressing reasons why all young people must come to recognise the incomparable value of lifelong learning.

What is at stake?

The OECD has acknowledged the importance of lifelong learning in achieving a range of educational, social and economic policy objectives since at least 1990, and the supporting arguments – particularly the economic ones – are now well known. The gathering momentum of globalisation and trade liberalisation, the ageing of populations and the changing nature of work all present an unprecedented challenge to the developed nations. It is increasingly evident that the distribution of employment opportunities is changing, with many unskilled jobs disappearing. And as people switch jobs more often – within OECD countries, it is estimated that roughly 18 per cent of workers have been in their present employment for less than a year – more frequent renewal of knowledge and skills is needed.

This rationale has now been articulated so often that it has lost much of its scare value. A counter-argument against the "prevailing orthodoxy" has also emerged – that states and employers are using the rhetoric of lifelong learning primarily to make workers more flexible and employable while ignoring structural problems such as continuing high unemployment and the increasing proportion of poorly paid, routine and insecure jobs.

One of the leading protagonists in this debate, Professor Frank Coffield of Newcastle University in England, has said: "In 1972, Edgar Faure, the former French prime minister [...] proposed 'lifelong learning as the master concept for educational policies in the years to come'. It has not happened; instead, flexibility has become the master concept in Western societies and Faure's enlightened, democratic vision of lifelong learning has been largely and unfairly forgotten" (Coffield, 1999).

OECD governments have, however, consistently seen the drive against educational underachievement and failure – and the new emphasis on lifelong learning – as more than a means to an economic end. Some politicians undoubtedly believe that "education is the best economic policy we have" (Blair, 1998). Nevertheless, none of the eight countries involved in this study considers lifelong learning to be synonymous with occupational training and retraining. In general, they would agree that it embraces "individual and social development of all kinds and in all settings – formally in schools, vocational, tertiary and adult education institutions, and non-formally, at home, at work and in the community" (OECD, 1996).

But OECD countries are certainly aware of the costs of failing to become educated, and staying educated. The fact is that educational failure and inflexibility has become punitive for the individual, in terms of unemployment or low earnings, a heavy burden for education systems, in terms of wasted resources, and harmful for society as a whole, in terms of reduced economic competitiveness and social cohesion (OECD, 1998a). As the OECD Council Meeting at Ministerial Level recognised in 1997: "High and persistent unemployment and low pay affecting significant sections of the working age population risk becoming threats to the social fabric unless they are addressed effectively and in good time."

Anyone who questions that analysis should consider the following points that help to explain why the "prevailing orthodoxy" has evolved:

- *Globalisation*: In 1993 it was estimated that there were 37 000 multinationals and 170 000 affiliates. What does that mean for individual countries? David Blunkett, the Education Secretary for England and Wales, likes to answer that question by recalling a statement by the chief executive of an international bank that had branches in 68 countries. If one of the countries did not provide sufficiently skilled people, the bank would simply look elsewhere for its key staff, he said. Now that new information and communications technology enables companies to draw on expertise from all over the world that threat is becoming more substantial with each passing year.

- *Demography*: The proportion of the OECD population aged 65 and over is expected to increase from 18.9 per cent in 1980 to 27.6 per cent in 2020. This shift will deliver the equivalent of a "demographic shock" – beginning around 2005 – to a large number of OECD countries, including Germany, Japan and, to a lesser extent, the United States (OECD, 1998a). It is therefore vital that the reduced proportions of young people are as well educated and trained as possible. Otherwise the financial burdens may prove intolerable. Canada, for example, estimates that it will lose more than US$4 billion over the working lives of nearly 137 000 youths who dropped out of secondary schools instead of graduating with the class of 1989.

But it is indeed the changing nature of *work* that now makes lifelong learning – that begins in schools rather than young adulthood – so imperative. In recent years it has been increasingly clear that OECD countries are becoming "learning economies" that are largely dependent on the creation and manipulation of knowledge information and ideas. By 2010 it is estimated that industrial workers may account for no more than 10-15 per cent of the total labour force in advanced OECD countries. It is, however, expected that there will be a strong, and potentially unsatisfied, demand for highly-skilled professional, technical, administrative and managerial staff (at least one of the countries involved in this study, Ireland, has already experienced acute skills shortages).

Furthermore, technological progress and the demands of this new knowledge economy mean that qualifications are becoming obsolete more quickly than ever. Linear careers are disappearing and by 2010 many of today's 18-year-olds will be doing a job that has not yet been invented. Moreover, they will be using skills that do not currently exist. In other words, the challenges of today's stick-shift world require a level of knowledge and expertise that cannot be acquired without effort, even by the most able students (Claxton, 1999).

19

Motivation and drop-out

In recent years OECD countries have been investing about US$1 trillion per annum in education – between 4.5 and 9 per cent of their GDP – and waves of education reform have washed around the globe. Curricula have been reformed, teacher training has been overhauled, evaluation and inspection services have been restructured, and many more university places have been provided. This has led to some significant progress. On average, children are now receiving one more year of education than they did in the mid-1980s and many more are obtaining university degrees.

Nevertheless, there is still widespread dissatisfaction with educational outcomes and the general level of student motivation in many countries. Some nations, particularly in the West, feel they have slipped back – at least relative to other countries – and this view appears to have been confirmed by international surveys such as the Third International Mathematics and Science Study (OECD, 1998*b*; TIMMS, 1996 and 1997). It found that children in Far Eastern countries such as Japan, Korea and Singapore were significantly ahead of the children of most other nations – in maths and science at least.

Japan and Korea are by no means complacent, however. Their children may be at the top of the world tables in two of the subject areas that are considered vital for economic success, but as this book will make clear, even they are concerned about the growing proportion of students who are truanting or dropping out of secondary school. Japan acknowledges that it has more than 100 000 school truants and that an increasing number of students are truanting for more than 30 days a year. Korea has a relatively low drop-out rate but is concerned about delinquency and the fact that only a third of students are satisfied with high school life.

It might seem that the new economic and occupational realities should provide sufficient motivation for young people to work hard at school and go on to become lifelong learners. However, all too many children and young people are either unable or unwilling to make the required effort – for myriad reasons. It may be that the deferment of gratification, which some study entails, runs counter to contemporary values ("I want it, and I want it now!"). Even the promise or expectation of later employment will therefore not be enough (Elliott and Hufton, 1999). As has already been pointed out, poverty is another factor that can prevent some children from fulfilling their potential. Others may have acute family and personal problems or drug dependencies. But many are simply unmotivated by their school experience.

Across the OECD, it is estimated that between 15 and 20 per cent of young people leave school without worthwhile qualifications. A slightly higher proportion (15 to 30 per cent) are classed as at risk of failing in school (OECD, 1995). They are consequently the ones least likely to secure well-paid and regular employment and provide a stable start in life for their own children. Surveys show that in countries such as Ireland and the UK, unemployment is more than twice as high for young people with below upper secondary education as it is for their peers with upper secondary or university education (OECD, 1997). This is not a new phenomenon, of course. Research has revealed that perhaps one-third of the adult population in OECD countries have acquired only minimum standards of literacy and numeracy, and many of them are unemployed.

Such statistics offer some insight into the scale of the challenges that national governments and education systems face but they can never provide an accurate gauge of teenagers' appetite for learning. A low drop-out rate does not necessarily signify that young people have a strong commitment to education that will develop into a passion for lifelong learning. It could, in fact, say more about the penalties for education failure within that society and the level of social control over the young. And a high drop-out rate, as in Iceland, may be partly attributable to the ready availability of jobs for teenagers, and the knowledge that secondary schooling can be completed at a later date. Unfortunately, no country yet has extensive data on the motivation levels of its children – although Finland should be able to produce such statistics relatively soon.

What can be done to motivate teenagers and raise educational standards?

International studies show that there is no single factor associated with educational success at the national level. Andy Green, an academic who has analysed the evolution of education systems in the East and the West, has concluded:

"None of the traditional indicators, whether class size, educational expenditure, selection, and grouping policies, teaching styles or time spent in learning particular subjects, correlates systematically with outcomes over a range of countries. Rather, the outcomes of the educational process in different countries are the result of a host of factors, some relating to the internal features of the education systems, and others to the social contexts. Countries which do relatively well in school education, such as France, Germany, Japan, South Korea, and Sweden, have certain things in common. As nations they emphasise educational achievement. They tend to have a 'learning culture' in which parents and teachers have high expectations of their children's educational achievements, where the education systems are designed to provide opportunities and motivation for all learners, and where the labour market, and society in general, reward those who do well in education. They have learned how to institutionalise high expectations for all through norm-reinforcing procedures and

21 |

practices such as national curricula and guidelines on teaching and assessment methods, professionally produced learning materials, interactive whole class teaching and so on" (Green, 1997).

But as we have pointed out, even countries such as Japan and Korea that appear to be motivating their children academically are well aware that they have troubles of their own. Although traditional, didactic schooling has brought them relative success they are conscious that individualism and creativity have not been sufficiently fostered.

In the East, as well as the West, it is increasingly accepted that schools, from early childhood onwards, should provide learning environments where learners like to be, where they experience a sense of self-worth, excitement, or challenge in learning. Children, before leaving the formal education system, must have "learned how to learn" under self-motivated and self-managed conditions. This assessment is endorsed by research findings, as the next chapter will demonstrate. The core learning processes that would pave the way for lifelong learning might include learning and thinking techniques, ways of organising knowledge, forms of expression, and interpersonal social relations. The list of cross-curriculum competencies drawn up by Trier and Peschar (1995) would also provide an excellent foundation: problem-solving, critical thinking, communication, democratic values, understanding of political processes, self-perception and self-confidence.

Many primary children must develop better basic skills in reading, writing and numbers in order to experience success in secondary school and later life. But there is also a clear need for some of the developments that are examined in detail in this book: more flexible curricula, individualised learning paths, better exploitation of new technologies, and more parity of esteem between vocational and academic studies (OECD, 1998a). The bridging of the vocational-academic gulf, which is under way in several of the countries studied, could do a great deal towards reconciling the educative and sorting functions of the education systems.

The challenge for education systems

As every country's school system grew out of different soil and has developed its own unique appearance there is no single set of "motivational" reforms that would be universally applicable or acceptable. But the evidence of this study – and a great deal of previous research – suggests that in the relatively near future many OECD countries will have to make radical changes to the way that children are taught and assessed.

School systems that are at present characterised by detailed and standardised curricula, classrooms organised by age divisions, fixed and narrow timetables, authoritarian teaching styles and rote learning seem destined to founder, sooner rather than later. This may seem to be an untenable contention given that this is precisely the profile of the most "successful" education systems in the world, but as the following chapters will demonstrate, even Far Eastern governments acknowledge that change is not only inevitable but desirable.

Standardised tests have been getting mixed reactions. On the one hand, some countries, such as the US, where standardised tests have traditionally not been in place, are now looking into the introduction of such tests in order to improve their educational outcomes. On the other hand, some educationists believe that the importance attached to standardised achievement tests will also have to be reduced. As they invariably involve the recall of memorised, factual knowledge in narrow areas of competence, they do little to develop the cross-curriculum skills, motivation and self-esteem that provide the best basis for lifelong learning. They can also have a devastatingly deleterious effect on the self-esteem of those they "weed out." As these tests and examinations currently exert a vice-like grip on the education systems of both the East and the West it is difficult to envisage how their power can be countered.

However, if curricula and assessment are to be reshaped this implies that the nature of teaching will also have to change. As the Canadian academic, Michael Fullan, has argued, the teaching profession, like other professions, is anxious about change and tends to resist it, preferring to maintain the status quo. OECD research has also indicated that some teachers are too ready to categorise pupils as either good or bad and do not believe it is their responsibility to change their students' attitudes (OECD, 1998a). Furthermore, it is hard to see how teachers can inculcate good lifelong learning habits in their students unless they, too, are lifelong learners.

But if so much more is to be expected of teachers they must be given something in return. Douglas Osler, Scotland's chief education adviser, acknowledged this in a recent statement about the importance of motivational teaching. "One of the answers is to make sure that teachers have more time to teach and more time to engage with pupils. The most critical factor in quality learning is quality teaching. If young people relate well to their teachers they will come, contribute and learn. No worksheet, no computer will do as well" (*Times Educational Supplement*, May 28, 1999).

Teachers will, however, need more than time if they are to create a more motivating school environment for children. They will also require something that they rarely get in some OECD countries – the whole-hearted support of politicians, employers, their local communities and parents.

The role of governments, employers, parents and communities

One of the more disheartening conclusions to emerge from this study is that even governments that support the concept of lifelong learning also advocate education policies that undermine the motivation and educational development of many children. Indeed, as an earlier OECD publication pointed out: "Among politicians and decision-makers there is too often only a superficial espousal of the grand principles and no real willingness to confront the consequences for action stemming from that espousal. Lifelong learning is one such principle that may well receive rhetorical support but not the corresponding radical agendas for governance and finance" (OECD, 1998a).

Politicians often criticise schools for failing to prevent drop-out, with some justification. Truants and drop-outs do frequently blame their behaviour on problems with teachers: most commonly a perceived lack of respect or a sense of injustice at being singled out or unfairly blamed. But judging by some research, it is not boring lessons but economic need or a national policy of forcing low-achievers to repeat a year that is more likely to cause students to drop out. This suggests that governments must shoulder at least part of the blame.

Governments must also face up to the fact that inequalities in educational careers among children from different social backgrounds have not diminished but remained remarkably stable, despite increases in the standard of living, rises in enrolment and reforms implemented to promote equal opportunities. Such inequalities inevitably feed through to the world of employment. Job-related adult education and training programmes tend to benefit the already well-educated. Those most in need of literacy skills training are not always reached. Employers could do more to redress this imbalance and some could also make it easier for schools to provide less-academically minded students with a taste of work experience. As the Danish chapter illustrates, such work experience does not necessarily make teenagers even more dissatisfied with school life – it can also be used as a "carrot" to keep them within the school system a little longer and make their studies more meaningful.

It is, however, the expectations of many parents, rather than pressure from employers, that can have the most stultifying effect on school systems. They invariably have their children's best interests at heart and can argue that they merely want the academic "passports" that society demands. But by attaching paramount importance to examination success and expecting their children to excel in traditional tasks they make it much harder for schools to experiment with new curricula, organisation or teaching methods. The Korean chapter explains how one innovative school managed to overcome parents' resistance to change, but as 90 per cent of its students go on to higher education this appears to be a fairly safe form of experimentation.

It is not only attitudes to schooling and qualifications that will have to be reshaped, however, if all young people are to be prepared for the stick-shift society. Governments, communities and employers will have to ensure that the number of obstacles preventing people from returning to education in adult life is kept to an absolute minimum. But some research indicates that even if that happens, perhaps one in five adults will resist all attempts to guide them into the lifelong learning net. As one study concluded: "Lack of motivation [...] may be the greatest barrier of all and its influence may be underestimated by the literature concentrating on the more easily visible barriers such as cost and entry qualifications" (Gorard *et al.*, 1998). Reducing the number of people who have no ambition to become learners will be extremely difficult, but as the next chapter on research findings will demonstrate, the problem is not insoluble.

Bibliography

BLAIR, T, Rt Hon (1998),
quoted in *The Learning Age: a Renaissance for a new Britain*, Stationery Office, Cm 3790, 9.

CLAXTON, G. (1999),
"A mind to learn: Education for the age of uncertainty", London University seminar paper.

COFFIELD, F. (1999),
"Breaking the Consensus: Lifelong Learning as Social Control", Lecture available from the Department of Education, Newcastle University, Newcastle.

ELLIOTT, J. and HUFTON, N. (1999),
"How can we raise achievement? A study of motivational factors in three countries", paper presented at American Education Research Association Conference.

GORARD, S. *et al.*, (1998),
"Society is not built by education alone: Alternative routes to the learning society", *Research in Post Compulsory Education*, Vol. 3, No 1.

GREEN, A. (1997),
The Times Educational Supplement, June 27.

KEGAN, R. (1994),
In *over our heads: the mental demands of modern life*, Harvard University Press, Cambridge, MA.

OECD (1995),
Our Children at Risk, Paris.

OECD (1996),
Lifelong Learning for All, Paris.

OECD (1997),
Literacy Skills for the Knowledge Society, Paris.

OECD (1998a),
Overcoming Failure at School, Paris.

OECD (1998b),
Education at a Glance – OECD Indicators, Paris.

TIMSS International Study Center (1996),
Mathematics achievement in the middle school years, International Association for the Evaluation of Education Achievement (IEA), United States.

TIMSS International Study Center (1997),
Mathematics achievement in the primary school years, International Association for the Evaluation of Education Achievement (IEA), United States.

TRIER, U.P. and PESCHAR, J. (1995),
"Cross-curriculum competencies: Rationale and strategy for developing a new indicator", in OECD, *Measuring What students Learn*, Paris.

Chapter 2

The Nature of Motivation: Some Key Insights

Many library shelves could be filled with the books and academic papers that psychologists and education researchers have produced on motivation over the past 50 years. We will therefore not attempt to provide the definitive overview of their research findings in this chapter. Neither will we try to describe and evaluate the many theories that have been advanced and debated. Our aim is merely to draw attention to a selection of significant, but often ignored, research findings that help to answer some key questions that are relevant to this study. What can be done to motivate disaffected students? Which school strategies are likely to stimulate the majority of adolescent students? How do teachers – and parents – affect students' motivation levels?

But before discussing the findings it is necessary to explain why psychological research into motivation has made relatively little impact on classroom practice – and why there is still no common unifying theory, or even a set of agreed principles. The principal stumbling block is that many types of factors can affect student motivation for good or ill. The United States National Research Council last year suggested that they could be:

- *Physical factors*: general state of health and nutrition, amount of sleep.
- *Psychological factors*: level of self-confidence, types of rewards, degree of interest from "significant others", such as teachers and parents.
- *Social factors*: level of support from family and peer group, number of distractions such as TV and sport, role models.
- *Educational factors*: the nature of the task being undertaken, its relevance, level of difficulty, and the way it is approached (National Research Council, 1999).

However, that list is by no means exhaustive. A nation's cultural attitudes towards education can also affect students' level of motivation. It is no secret that parents in Far Eastern countries drive their children to excel at school, believing that a good education is the best guarantee of upward mobility or financial security. What is less well-known is that in some countries, such as Finland, children have traditionally been brought up to believe that it is very important to become "an educated person". Furthermore, children of different cultures sometimes have to be motivated in different ways (these cultural themes will be explored at the end of this chapter).

Economic factors, such as the level of youth unemployment and the availability of student grants, may also have either a positive or negative impact on students' motivation, as may examination systems and assessment policies. But the US research council's central argument, that many variables muddy the motivational waters, is incontestable.

Intrinsic and extrinsic motivation

While this chapter will not be addressing theoretical issues it is important to understand the distinction that researchers make between intrinsic and extrinsic motivation. Intrinsically-motivated students undertake an activity "for its own sake, for the enjoyment it provides, the learning it permits, or the feelings of accomplishment it evokes" (Lepper, 1988). An extrinsically-motivated student, on the other hand, seeks "to obtain some reward or avoid some punishment external to the activity itself", such as grades, stickers, or teacher approval.

Intrinsically-motivated students are said to employ strategies that demand more effort and that enable them to process information more deeply. Extrinsically-motivated students, by contrast, are inclined to make the minimum effort to achieve an award. Older behaviourist perspectives on motivation assumed that teachers could manipulate children's engagement with schoolwork through the introduction of controls and rewards. However, research has tended to show that children usually revert to their original behaviour when the rewards stop. Furthermore, at least two dozen studies have shown that people expecting to receive a reward for completing a task – or for doing it successfully – do not perform as well as those who expect nothing. This appears to be true for children and adults, for males and females, for rewards of all kinds and for tasks ranging from memorising facts to designing collages.

This may be dispiriting news for the many schools around the world that offer a vast range of "prizes" – such as books or even hamburger restaurant vouchers – for good work or perfect attendance (none of the schools in our study resorted to such tactics). However, the positive effect of extrinsic rewards may not be immediately obvious. As N.L. Gage and D. Berliner have pointed out: "A skilled reader or piano player may appear to be motivated from within [...] [but] initially, the reading or piano playing may have been fostered by social approval from parents or teachers – a hug and lollipop for reading the words cat and hat, and a special celebration after the first recognisable song (Gage and Berliner, 1979)."

Some may see this as little more than a common sense analysis, an accusation that is often levelled at motivation theories. Survey findings that have resulted from motivation research have sometimes faced similar charges. It should also be borne in mind that much of the research into motivation has emanated from the United States and may therefore not be considered representative of other countries' experience. That may help to explain why the majority of the government officials and teachers in charge of the motivation projects we assessed seemed to have paid relatively little heed to research findings. Nevertheless, a search of the academic literature on motivation reveals that some light has been shed on the following issues.

What can be done to motivate disaffected students?

Dropping out is not a sudden event that happens in secondary school; it is the culmination of a process of disengagement from education that often begins in the infant class. The impressions that young children form about their abilities, based on messages from their family and school, can strongly influence their motivation to succeed. However, young children tend to maintain high expectations of success even after repeated failure; older students do not. And although younger children generally see virtually all effort as a good thing, older children view it as a "double-edged sword" (Ames, 1990). Failure that follows great effort can be much more damaging to their self-concept of ability than failure that results from minimal effort. Apparently lazy or unco-operative students may therefore be trying to protect their sense of self-worth.

Difficult-to-motivate students often benefit from individualised computer-based work because it enables them to make mistakes and correct them without losing face. Their self-esteem also grows as their mastery of the technology develops. However, new technology alone cannot solve the problem of disaffected students.

The evidence from the United States suggests that an effective drop-out prevention programme would ideally include the following characteristics: teachers with the authority to design courses/experiences; low student-teacher ratios; teachers attuned to students' needs; a low absentee, theft and drug-abuse environment; individualisation; an active role for students; emphasis on basic skills remediation; and readiness to tackle students' personal problems.

Barbara L. McCombs and James E. Pope, two specialists in motivating disaffected students, believe that: "Individuals are naturally motivated to learn when they do not have to fear failure, when they perceive what they are learning as being personally meaningful and relevant and when they are in respectful and supportive relationships with teachers" (McCombs and Pope, 1994). But McCombs and Pope emphasise that the most important common element of successful pro-grammes with troubled teenagers appears to be the quality of the relationship that are established between adults and young people. "It seems to matter les what is done than who does it and how [...]. Teachers who are best at reaching the most difficult to reach youth are those who are consistently upbeat and unafraid and have a consistent empathic regard for their students."

We encountered a surprisingly large number of these paragons during the course of our country visits. But as such teachers will always be in short supply i would perhaps be sensible to make secondary schools more "student friendly". A present there is often a serious mismatch between the organisation and curriculum of schools and the intellectual and emotional needs of adolescents.

In order to create a "psychological environment" that will increase student motivation, it would appear that schools should:

- Foster teamwork through group learning and problem-solving experiences.

- Replace social comparisons of achievement with self-assessment and evaluation techniques.

- Teach time-management skills and offer self-paced instruction when possible.

- Stress goal-setting and self-management (Maehr, 1991).

Other research suggests that children are likely to become enthusiastic lifelong learners if they have:

- An engaging curriculum.

- A safe, caring community in which to discover and create.

- A significant degree of choice about what and how and why they are learning.

Motivation is said to increase if students are asked to assume greater auton-omy and control over their lives and learning as they pass through secondary school (a view shared by many of the teachers and education professionals in the eight countries that took part in the OECD study). However, back in 1982 David Hargreaves, a British researcher, was already asserting that schools had become so obsessed with individual needs that they often overlooked their social function. He argued that personal identity develops in a social context and if schools did not give their pupils a sense of belonging they would turn elsewhere – perhaps to a disaffected adolescent group – to meet this basic human need.

Twenty years earlier, J.S. Coleman expressed concern that US high schools were allowing adolescent sub-cultures to divert energies into athletics and social activi-ties. "In fact the high school seems to do more than allow these sub-cultures to dis-courage academic achievement; it aids them in doing so [...]. One might speculate on the possible effects of city-wide or state-wide 'scholastic fairs' composed of academic games and tournaments between schools" (Coleman, 1960).

If anything, sport has assumed even more importance in most developed nations since Coleman aired that anxiety. But there is still relatively little interest in academic tournaments. In fact, in not only America but other OECD countries an anti-academic adolescent peer culture tends to undermine any drive to improve education standards. Raising and maintaining students' motivation levels is therefore a never-ending process that requires a huge amount of commitment and creativity from teachers. As the following chapters will show, most of the teachers who took part in this study displayed the necessary dedication. In fact, in some cases there seemed to be a danger of "professional burn-out" if they maintained their present work-rate.

How teachers and teaching approaches can affect students' motivation levels

The basic message that has emerged from many studies is that students expect to learn if their teachers expect them to learn. In the late 1960s and 70s a number of observational studies of classrooms were conducted to determine how teachers interact with students that they perceived to be high or low achievers. One study found that about one-third of classroom teachers showed patterns of highly differentiated behaviour. They called on low achievers less often to answer questions or perform demonstrations. The teachers also waited less time for them to answer questions, praised them less frequently after successful responses, criticised them more often for incorrect responses, and did not help them when they failed by providing clues or asking follow-up questions (Brophy and Good, 1974).

Defining tasks in terms of short-term goals can help students to associate effort with success, but of course long-term goals are also needed if students are to become lifelong-learners. Tasks that involve "a moderate amount of discrepancy or incongruity" can also generate intrinsic motivation by stimulating students' curiosity (Lepper, 1988). Although no subject can be made interesting to every child, intrinsic motivation can be enhanced by project-based learning, which enables small groups of students to work together on extended exercises.

Discovery learning, an approach developed by cognitive psychologists to encourage students to discover for themselves the concepts and connections that underlie a body of knowledge, also has many advocates. But discovery-learning experiences must strike the right balance between simplicity and complexity. Research on curiosity suggests that people lose interest in a task if it is so simple it becomes boring, or so complex that it appears chaotic and meaningless. Achieving the right balance is not easy, of course, particularly in a large class. But the research literature suggests that teachers not only need to be able to bring off such balancing acts; they should ideally know what drives every child in their class. "When students are [...] primarily concerned with avoiding failure in their lives, they make different choices than when their predominant motive is to succeed" (Gage and Berliner, 1979).

Praise is another problematic issue. Although it is important to avoid "put-downs", rewarding children with praise can sometimes be counter-productive. Some researchers believe this can create a growing dependence on securing someone else's approval. It is also claimed that extroverts can be motivated more by blame than by praise, while introverts are more motivated by praise. Furthermore, teachers who try to encourage intrinsic values by praising students for engaging in activities such as writing poetry outside the classroom may actually discourage them from continuing. The phenomenon has been described as the "over-justification effect". It is thought to occur because the addition of rewards devalues a justifiable activity.

The awarding of grades for schoolwork has generated even more debate among researchers. Some studies have indicated that they have a detrimental effect on creative thinking, staying-on rates and general interest in learning. In one Israeli study, 11-year-olds were given either written feedback on their tests, a graded mark or both. The performance of the group who received only comments increased by one third, while that of the other two groups declined. However, the extent to which students become intrinsically engaged in a task or subject often depends on whether or not they have achieved the hoped-for grades. Being successful in one's studies promotes emotions such as hope, pride, and joy that increase enthusiasm and an appreciation for what one is learning. But this does not necessarily justify competitive testing. Rewarding students on the basis of improvement over their own past performance has also proved to be an effective incentive. However, this was not a preferred tactic in the schools that took part in this study. Several had introduced records of achievement so that vocational students could chart their progress, but this was a much more subtle form of reward.

The influence of parents

Some American research has suggested that motivation levels are affected not only by the characteristics of the home background, such as social class, but the number of children in the family, and the mother's age. At least one study claimed that firstborn children tend to have a stronger drive to achieve. But such research has often generated conflicting evidence.

It is also by no means clear whether parents should promise rewards to induce children to do well in school. As we explained earlier, they can have positive and negative consequences. However, some strategies are unquestionably beneficial. "When parents nurture their children's natural curiosity about the world by welcoming their questions, encouraging exploration, and familiarising them with resources that can enlarge their world, they are giving their children the message that learning is worthwhile and frequently fun and satisfying. When children are raised in a home that nurtures a sense of self-worth, competence, autonomy, and self-efficacy, they will be more apt to accept the risks inherent in learning" (Lumsden, 1994).

The influence of parents does appear to vary greatly from one society to another, however. A team of Asian and American researchers who investigated the reasons why Japanese and Chinese children consistently outperformed their US peers found that several of the important factors were unrelated to school or classroom organisation (Stevenson and Stigler, 1992). Asian parents were far less inclined to tolerate mediocre performance than their American counterparts and they encouraged their children to spend much more time studying out of school hours. This finding has been substantiated by a number of other studies, including more recent research by Eaton and Dembo (1997). After comparing the performance and attitudes of Asian Americans and Caucasian Americans they concluded that fear of failure, stemming from family pressures, best explained the Asian Americans' higher workrate.

Complications and conundrums

As Dutch researchers pointed out last year, the relationship between motivation and attainment is by no means straightforward (Kuyper *et al.*, 1999). Research has shown that not only low but unduly high motivation may lead to lower achievement than might be expected on the basis of aptitudes. Psychologists have, however, been aware of this phenomenon for many years. As Gage and Berliner pointed out in 1979: "Perseverance in an inappropriate situation can be, to a clinical psychologist, a sign of a problem. Because of neurotic needs to achieve, a child may spend inordinate amounts of time on an insoluble problem. Then high motivation becomes a hindrance rather than an aid to learning" (Gage and Berliner, 1979).

One further complication is that although strong motivation and high self-esteem are sometimes seen as synonymous, children with high self-esteem may not actually be the most motivated and successful students. Analysis of the Third International Mathematics and Science Study (TIMSS) data has shown that although English 14-year-olds scored slightly below the international average in maths, 93 per cent of them believed they were doing well in the subject (Keys and Fernandes, 1997). However, in Singapore, which was placed top in the TIMSS ranking, only 57 per cent of children said that they were good at maths – an outcome that may not be altogether surprising given the emphasis that Eastern cultures tend to place on personal modesty.

Another recent study of children's motivation and attainment levels in Russia, the United States and England also found that Russian children did much better in maths tests than the US and English children even though they had a lower opinion of their academic ability (Elliott, 1999). The Russian teenagers were also much more likely to believe that "being clever" rather than "working hard" was important for success in schoolwork. This contradicts the common view that children are more likely to be motivated, and reach a higher attainment level, if they believe that effort, rather than ability, is what matters most. However, the researchers found that the Russians worked harder than the American or English children all the same and did recognise that effort was important. They also liked school more and the majority said that their main goal was to become an "educated person". The English and American teenagers, however, said that their primary objective was to obtain qualifications.

The belief that students only go to school to get qualifications that will secure them a well-paid job militates against the intrinsic valuing of education for two reasons. "It deprives young people of the feeling that what they are doing *now* is important. All the rewards seem to be somewhere in the future. Secondly, it deprives society of the understanding that learning has value in itself and not just as a saleable commodity. This greatly reduces the range of knowledge worth having, and creates a population of narrowly-educated citizens" (Tye, 1985).

This again suggests that national cultures may have a bigger effect on children's motivation levels and educational achievement than is generally recognised. It is also a reminder of the special challenges that teachers and would-be reformers face in some countries. Not only do they have to cope with a bewilderingly complex array of physical, psychological, social and educational factors that may affect motivation levels. They also have to try to counter unhelpful national or peer cultures. There are, however, strategies that all governments can adopt to nudge students on to the path to lifelong learning. This will be the focus of the next chapter.

Bibliography

AMES, C. (1990),
  "Motivation: what teachers need to know", Teachers College Record Vol. 91, No. 3, Spring.

BROPHY, J.E. and GOOD, T.L. (1974),
  Teacher – student relationships: causes and consequences, Holt, Rinehart and Winston, New York.

COLEMAN, J.S. (1960),
  "The adolescent sub-culture and academic achievement", *American Journal of Sociology*.

EATON, M J. and DEMBO, M.H. (1997),
  "Differences in the motivational beliefs of Asian-American and Non-Asian students", *Journal of Educational Psychology*, Vol. 89 (3).

ELLIOTT, J. (1999),
  "How can we raise achievement? A study of motivational factors in three countries", paper presented at the American Educational Research Association conference.

GAGE, N L. and BERLINER, D. (1979),
  Educational Psychology, Rand McNally.

KEYS, W. and FERNANDES, C. (1997),
  Third International Mathematics and Science Study, First National Report (Part 2), National Foundation for Educational Research.

KUYPER *et al.* (1999),
  "Motivation, meta-cognition and self-regulation as predictors of long-term educational attainment", paper presented to the American Educational Research Association conference.

LEPPER, M. (1988),
  "Motivational considerations in the study of instruction", *Cognition and Instruction*.

LUMSDEN, L. (1994),
  "Student motivation to learn", ERIC *Digest*, No. 92.

MAEHR, M.L. (1991),
  "Changing the Schools: a word to school leaders about enhancing student investment in learning", paper presented to the American Educational Research Association Conference.

McCOMBS, B.L. and POPE, J.E. (1994),
  "Motivating Hard to Reach students", American Psychological Association.

NATIONAL RESEARCH COUNCIL (1999),
  "Improving student Learning: a strategic plan for education research and utilisation."

STEVENSON, H.W. and STIGLER, J.W. (1992),
  The Learning Gap: Why our schools are failing and what we can learn from Japanese and Chinese education, Summit Books, New York.

TYE, B.B. (1985),
  Multiple Realities: A study of 13 American high schools, University Press of America, Lanham, MD.

Chapter 3

Policy Dimensions and Approaches

All the countries in this study have policies that refer specifically to promoting lifelong learning, though these are not the monopoly of education ministries. Life-long learning, often seen as incremental educational growth, may also be conceptualised from a holistic position that includes social welfare, health and labour-market considerations. During our study visits we were struck by the tension evident in two-pronged government policies that were not only attempting to address current problems but respond to predictions about a country's long-term economic, political, cultural and social future. In Japan, for example, future trends such as globalisation, the information age, developments in science and technology and demographic shifts are placed alongside current concerns with drop-outs, truancy, bullying and violence in schools.

Inevitably, the impact of government policies varied and we would echo the statement in a 1999 OECD report (OECD, 1999): "Governments are not omnipotent." We also noted the distance between government policies and the projects in the various schools we visited. Even in countries where there is strong central control of the education service, national policies sometimes appeared to follow in the wake of individual school or province initiatives. In other instances it was a government initiative that stimulated change at the grassroots.

Various government reports, statements of intent and pieces of legislation refer directly to motivation. In some cases, policies are aimed at motivating young people towards government-defined goals through more diversified learning opportunities. In others, efforts are designed to demotivate young people from engaging in anti-social behaviour.

What emerged as the two most important concepts underpinning policies were individuality and diversity. Individuality is associated with student-centred education and finds expression in curricular arrangements, teaching strategies, student assessment and even school design. These must be considered alongside student services including learning support, guidance and counselling, and health and welfare provision. The growing diversity, on the other hand, is reflected in greater choice of institutions, courses, learning methods and modes of assessment. In both Iceland and Japan, for example, our attention was drawn to new distance-learning courses that were providing second-chance options for growing numbers of adult learners.

In many countries, drop-out rates are used as a key indicator of student motivation. However, our study revealed that the two are not always closely related. For example, a booming economy and expansion of the jobs market are encouraging students in some countries to make a premature exit from the education system. Equally, a very rigid system that discourages students from dropping out and returning at a later date can ensure that even young people with relatively low levels of motivation stay on in school.

Balancing theoretical studies with authentic, first-hand experience

"Zest for learning" is a phrase that captures the need for students to develop commitment and enthusiasm for lifelong learning. This objective permeates government documents in Japan and Norway. In Japan, enabling students to learn, think, make judgements, act independently and be more adept at problem-solving lies at the heart of this. In Norway, it is echoed in the statement (Ministry of Church, Education and Research, 1994) "[...] the aim of education is to expand the individual's capacity to perceive and to participate, to experience, to empathise and to excel". These goals are the product of many forces, including the demands of influential employers' organisations, the recognition of the ever-changing characteristics of a diverse youth culture, and the reconceptualisation of curricula to take account of the perceived needs of citizens in the 21st century. These pressures have triggered proposals for redefining the content of traditional subjects and the ways that subjects relate to each other. In the eight countries surveyed, these find expression in the extension of school-based studies into the local community and curriculum integration.

Curriculum integration is a loose term that covers a variety of arrangements. It may refer to the integration of vocational and general modules. It may also refer to thematic studies, such as environmental education and citizenship education, that cross subject boundaries. From a different perspective, literacy and numeracy have been identified as cross-curricular themes. What is clear is that conventional subjects in schools are very robust. They have clearly differentiated boundaries and specialist teachers and teaching materials, especially in those countries having government-approved textbooks. Introducing curriculum integration in any form is not easy and may require legislative direction. Thus, in Norway, it has been decreed that all upper secondary students must engage in at least one cross-disciplinary project each year to develop such skills as co-operation, creativity and analytical thinking.

"Learning by doing" is a feature of the open youth education programme and the production school programme in Denmark. It is also an element of alternative curricula for disadvantaged groups in Norway and Finland. But theoretical studies have not been rejected in these programmes: they have become integral to skills-based courses.

That schools, within their walls, cannot provide all of the learning experiences judged to be important for secondary students is obvious. There is a need for schools to provide periods of work experience for all students following both vocational and general courses. Virtually all governments now appear to recognise this, but some are more committed to this objective than others. In Finland, for example, it is now mandatory for all three-year vocational courses to include a six-month workplacement.

The argument for students to be prepared for their roles as active citizens by engaging in extra-curricular activities in local communities is equally strong. Government policies in all of the countries acknowledge the importance of out-of-school activities for motivating young people. They vary from the individualised extra-curricular activities in Korea, to work experience for vocational students in Finland, and for all students in England. Integrating the experiences that students gain from these activities poses new challenges for teachers and calls for changes in attitudes to education among employers and parents. These strategies have implications for redefining the roles of schools. They could also change profoundly teachers' perceptions of the nature of their work.

Adapting teaching methods

Teachers are powerful role models for adolescents. At their best they embody the principles of lifelong learning. They demonstrate that they are active lifelong learners and that they are fulfilling themselves through their own learning activities. Without this example many students are unlikely to be motivated to become lifelong learners.

The challenge for teachers in vocational and general programmes is to capture the attention of all their students while seeking to emphasise individualised approaches to learning. The one-way knowledge transmission model, stereotyped as teachers reading and interpreting textbooks to whole classes of passive students, has not disappeared but governments are challenging such practices, believing that they are demotivating and thoroughly inappropriate in a lifelong learning culture.

However, one of the strongest challenges to the model has not come from government policies but from the rapid dissemination of new technologies to schools

39

and, just as importantly, to students' homes. New technologies, used for entertainment, the gathering of information and for interpersonal communication are highly motivational. They have challenged the teacher and the approved textbook as sources of authoritative and up-to-date knowledge and they have brought long-accepted teaching methods into question.

Other pressures have combined with the new technologies to cause governments to address teaching methods. There are calls for changes in the school-defined roles and inter-personal relationships of teachers and students. In all eight countries there are statements recommending student-centred approaches. Implicit in these is the requirement for teachers to adapt learning as far as possible to meet the needs of individual students. Classroom work that is ill-matched to children's abilities and interests is unlikely to motivate them in either the short or long term. Furthermore, teachers are encouraged to become "enablers" rather than transmitters of knowledge. Active learning and co-operative learning, distance learning and computer-assisted learning are all parts of the argument. That students themselves have a teaching role is explicit in co-operative methods that focus on problem-solving. Such developments are vitally important in the context of motivation for lifelong learning for *all* students.

It is assumed that there is a readiness for change on the part of not only teachers and students but schools and their communities. However, if new teaching methods and forms of learning are not mirrored in examinations they will not become universally accepted.

Introducing student-centred assessment

Some governments have recognised that there is a need for new forms of assessment that are compatible with student-centred approaches to teaching and learning. Assessment and learning go hand-in-hand: what can be learned can be assessed and what can be assessed can be learned. However, assessment fulfils many functions. Conceptually, there is an enormous distance between a one-off test that ends a phase of learning and assessment that provides the launch pad for the next learning experience. Assessment in lifelong learning should ease the transition between phases and give the student the confidence, enthusiasm and commitment to face new learning challenges.

That examinations can motivate students to study for long hours inside and outside of school is evident in Japan and Korea. Indeed, cram schools have blossomed in Japan to the extent that the government is seeking ways to curb their excesses. But examination systems cannot be reformed easily and there is often strong resistance to any talk of change. Advocates of reform are concerned not only with the polarising influence of exams but the effect that both success and failure have on students' aspirations (OECD, 1999):

"For both qualified and disqualified students, assessment underpins not only grades and diplomas but also self-image, and this is consistently reinforced by its effect on social reputation. Over time, students who qualify consider themselves able and worthy, while the reverse holds for those who do not qualify who voluntarily temper their social aspirations accordingly."

In a lifelong learning context the results of end-of-course examinations are but one component in a student's overall achievement. If no account is taken by employers and educational institutions of other curricular and extra-curricular experiences and achievements then the value attached to them by students is likely to be substantially reduced. As work experience, community experience and a diverse range of extra-curricular school activities are advocated by governments for their learning gains these should be reflected in any assessment of a student's progress. Government proposals for progress files or records of achievement (as in England), portfolios (in Ireland), training logs (in Norway) and individual log books (in Denmark) acknowledge the importance of information that recognises the range of student achievement and supplements conventional examinations. Promoting the use of such reports for all students rather than only with those following vocational courses is a natural policy step.

The introduction of modular courses and new methods of studying them, such as distance learning, have made examination arrangements more flexible. In Iceland and Norway, where such arrangements are well-developed, students can choose when to be examined and also when to complete their studies. The introduction of part-qualifications, as in Norway, is an interesting aspect of this. Some modular arrangements provide greater opportunities to resit examinations and for students to self-evaluate their progress over time. More frequent feedback and more opportunities to demonstrate success are seen as motivating for students. They provide links with incentive systems and appraisal systems used by some employers.

Bridging the vocational and general divide

The tradition of distinguishing sharply between non-vocational courses leading to tertiary education and vocational courses leading to jobs has forced teenagers in some countries to make early decisions about suitable pathways. In other countries where vocational education has a particularly low status the decisions have been made for them.

In countries that fall into the former category, governments are seeking to reform institutions, curricula and examinations in response to the general uncertainty about future employment patterns and the pressures to increase participation rates in upper secondary and higher education. Students are increasingly being encouraged to keep their educational and career options open and to make choices only after obtaining the best advice available.

Delayed choice of study route lies at the heart of Denmark's reform 2000 where the strengthening of general courses in vocational programmes has opened up new pathways to higher education. In England, examinations reform has allowed students to choose subjects drawn from both general and vocational programmes. Greater choice requires students to be more self-reliant. It also encourages students to take their studies seriously and to consider carefully the consequences of their choices for their future careers and lifestyles.

Governments are also seeking answers to a difficult question: should there be a core curriculum bridging the divide and, if so, what should this comprise? Should it be driven by notions of a classical curriculum where the emphasis is on knowledge defined by subjects or should it be driven by a formulation of basic, transferable skills? Should the core comprise conventional subjects or should it be made up of integrated courses or projects or thematic studies?

In England, pupils aged 11 to 14 must study 11 national curriculum subjects. From 14 to 16, however, there are only six compulsory subjects for most pupils, and one or two of those can be dropped to make way for a structured programme of work-related learning. There is therefore considerable freedom from 14 to 16 to study other vocational or academic subjects. There are no national curriculum requirements post-16. In Finland and Norway, students are required to accumulate a fixed amount of credit gained from successfully completing modular courses. These modules may be taught in conventional or innovative ways and the credit so gained can be carried from one school to another. Distance – learning modules also carry credit that may be accepted by other institutions. In Norway and Finland, students may interrupt their studies and they can decide within specified time limits how and when they will try to gain university entry or vocational qualifications.

The governments in our study acknowledge that opening up choice of institution, course pattern, learning methods and modes of assessment complicates the educational system for the immature learner. Choices are challenging and may be threatening: they bring uncertainty and risk. Hence, the attention paid to guidance and counselling in making lifelong learning a reality.

Enhancing guidance and counselling services

Guidance and counselling services have figured prominently in recent educational policies in all eight countries. Inevitably, reforms that have opened up more diversified study opportunities and access to new types of employment have been accompanied by proposals for assisting students to make appropriate choices. The merging of vocational and general education in single institutions or the opening up of more specialist institutions poses difficult questions about pathways for students. They not only need expert advice about courses to follow but also about the changing labour market.

From a lifelong learning perspective, students require advice especially at major points of transition. An ill-considered choice at 16 or 18 can have long-lasting consequences, particularly if the decision is to quit school or college. There are many instances of people studying at night school or paying for private training in order to escape from a job that is making them unhappy but this is obviously a far from ideal motivation for returning to education.

Many students, especially the least advantaged, need counselling and support services throughout their studies and this has been recognised in government policies. As with course design and assessment arrangements, these services must be student-friendly. Advisers and counsellors have a pivotal role in motivating adolescents. The importance of a highly personalised support service is evident in proposals in England for personal advisers available to all young people over the age of 13. In Finland, all upper comprehensive schools have counsellors providing advice on studying, career paths and ways of applying for the next stage of education. Norway has given upper secondary students a statutory right to both counselling and career guidance. In Denmark, students in the open youth education programme are supported by personal counsellors.

Improving the infrastructure

The success of government policies is heavily dependent on the existence of an appropriate infrastructure. Innovations are unlikely to succeed if institutions are not ready to accept them. Even excellent government proposals will not be accepted if they require funding that is not available or forthcoming. Senior staff and teachers in schools are also unlikely to support proposals for which they have not been prepared. Lacking in-service training, teachers may misinterpret government intentions and policies and be unable to adopt new roles.

For some students, motivation for learning is closely linked with financial support for their studies. Not all countries provide free secondary education and those that do sometimes expect students to buy their textbooks and other learning materials. For needy students, some countries provide free meals and health care, subsidised transport to and from school and charge no fees. Some provide assistance with accommodation for those students who have to move away from home to follow specialised courses.

43

Another important infra-structural component is the relationship between schools and local communities. In Scandinavian countries, employers, unions and the local community are often represented on school governing bodies. But they have other important new roles. Clearly, the work-experience and community-experience schemes referred to earlier would not get off the ground without close partnerships between schools and many other agencies. Adults in the organisations that offer work-placements often have an important influence on student motivation. Schools need to ensure that external organisations are fully aware of this responsibility. Just as teachers are important role models for lifelong learning so are the employers and employees in these organisations.

Most important of all, radical proposals for change at governmental or school levels must take into account parental expectations of how courses are taught and assessed. In countries with strong private educational sectors, wealthier parents can supplement or opt out of state schooling. Many parents have strong views about how schools should be run, but they must be encouraged to come to terms with the lifelong learning needs of their offspring. This includes supporting policy-makers seeking to introduce reforms. Some parents struggle to do this, of course, because they have their own unfilled learning needs. But in many OECD countries, governments are now trying to ensure that more bridges are built between the school and home. One of the universal teachers' adages is "the parents you most need to see are the ones who never come to the school". However, this may become less true as a result of initiatives such as Ireland's home-school community liaison programme. For the past 10 years it has been requiring schools in disadvantaged areas to deploy a teacher – full-time – to the task of developing home-school-community relationships.

Establishing environments for lifelong learning

School design can affect the amount of space a student has to develop individually and socially. Students – and teachers – may be more or less motivated by the layout and design of classroom, workshop and laboratory equipment and furnishings. Ethos and school culture are recognised by governments as important contextual factors contributing to student motivation.

Clearly, school design has to be responsive to both the dynamic and complicated contemporary youth culture and the future needs of both students and communities. Increasingly, new technologies are posing fresh challenges for the design of schools. Cyber-cafes are becoming as necessary as sports facilities, accommodation for guidance and counselling services as important as libraries, professional workshops and conference rooms for staff as important as lounges.

For policy-makers, falling enrolments offer opportunities for reorganising space within schools. There is also a need for institutions specialising in music, technology or languages, as well as for schools with facilities for groups with particular special needs. Residential accommodation must be designed for disadvantaged groups and, in some circumstances, for ordinary students.

Out-of-school approaches

Important though the physical lay-out of a school is, it is the psychological environment that is a more important determinant of student motivation levels, judging by the research evidence presented in Chapter 2. Some young people never find what they need inside the gates of a school, irrespective of whether the premises are spacious or cramped, old or new. That is why the sort of schemes that the Irish government has set up for recent school-leavers and unemployed adults are so important.

Many unqualified 15 to 18-year-olds appeared to be blossoming in the 100 out-of-school centres that operate under the YOUTHREACH scheme. Like schools, these centres place strong emphasis on literacy, numeracy and IT. But some of the YOUTHREACH participants believe that the programme offers them other things that were lacking in the schools they left as "failures" – trust, choice and respect. The Irish government has also made a substantial investment in its Vocational Training Opportunities Schemes (VTOS) that provides a second chance for over-21s who are either unemployed or dependent on social benefits. The opportunity to use and master state-of-the-art IT equipment and obtain further education qualifications are two of the important attractions of this scheme.

Of course, Ireland is not alone in seeing the merit of such programmes, which can sometimes be daringly innovative and tap a different range of funding sources. Throughout Scandinavia there are government-funded programmes that aim to give young unemployed people not only marketable skills but a more positive attitude towards learning and life. Finland, for example, has a network of workshops where young adults can repair cars, restore furniture and develop dozens of other skills. There may always be a need for such enterprises unless youth unemployment levels drop substantially. However, the ultimate hope must be that the school reforms discussed in this report will mean that fewer young people will have to be caught by programmes such as YOUTHREACH and the Finnish workshops.

The involvement of local and regional government

Local and regional education authorities do not have prominent roles in the policy-making described in this study but in several countries they do make a significant contribution. Although the power of England's local education authorities has been substantially curtailed over the past 10 years they have been closely involved in each of the three projects described in the UK chapter. In one instance they initiated a project, in another they took part in a government-funded scheme and in the third, they worked in tandem with an innovative head teacher. Local authorities in Ireland have also been providing essential support for the YOUTHREACH and VTOS schemes described in the previous section.

Similarly, in Scandinavia, municipalities have provided essential funding and equipment for projects. For example, a county municipality had given one of the Norwegian schools, Nesodden, laptop computers for no fewer than 55 students and 20 teachers. These have enabled the school to explore new teaching and learning approaches. In Finland, where much more power has been devolved to the municipalities in recent years, schools were working very closely with local politicians and education administrators. The Finnish local authorities accepted that it was important to motivate children for lifelong learning but other concerns appeared to be higher on their agendas. One municipality was primarily concerned with rising enrolments, the other two with high unemployment and its social consequences.

In the Far East, state education systems are largely government-controlled. Nevertheless, some of the Japanese and Korean local authorities made more than token contributions to the efforts to motivate students. Korea's South Choong-Chung province had even initiated and pioneered student-centred reforms that aim to reduce the emphasis on rote learning and foster problem-solving, analytical work and creativity. But as the country chapters show, in Japan and Korea it was sometimes difficult to differentiate between local authorities who were really stimulating change and those that were merely echoing or rephrasing government policy statements. In both the East and the West it seemed that there was more scope for genuinely innovative local authority involvement in projects designed to increase student motivation.

Conclusion

It is sometimes argued that apparent similarities in policies and practice between countries mask essential differences. Certainly, the term "lifelong learning", although frequently highlighted as the basis for government policies, means different things from country to country and even from one institution to another within countries. In much the same way, the expression "motivating adolescents" is seen by some institutions as being a response to truancy, drop out and anti-social behaviour. Others associate it with either students at risk or those with special needs. And yet others focus on particular groups such as boys or immigrants.

46

Hence, it is not surprising to find differences between government policies and institutional practices. There is wide scope for interpretation in statements of intent and legislation. Notice the optimism in this statement from an English consultation paper: "Our vision is to build a new culture of learning which will underpin national competitiveness and personal prosperity and help build a cohesive society" (Department for Education and Employment, 1999). Any new culture of learning must inevitably demand changes in the culture of schools and in the attitudes towards education that are displayed by influential stakeholders – parents, employers, community organisations and regional and local governments. Schools must come to terms with the full implications of lifelong learning, and motivating all adolescents to become lifelong learners is a massive challenge. In the next chapter we shall present findings from our study visits and highlight the effectiveness of innovations at the local level.

47

Bibliography

DEPARTMENT FOR EDUCATION AND EMPLOYMENT (1999),
"Learning to succeed: a new framework for post-16 learning", White Paper, Cm. 4392, London.

MINISTRY OF CHURCH, EDUCATION AND RESEARCH (1994),
Core Curriculum for Primary, Secondary and Adult Education in Norway, Oslo.

OECD (1999),
Innovating Schools, Paris.

Chapter 4

Initiatives to Improve Student Motivation:
Features and Outcomes

A great deal is known about the ocean currents that have a significant effect on the world's climate. But the "currents" of opinion that help to determine the education policy-making climate are often more of a mystery. Why should countries as far apart and disparate as Japan and Norway suddenly be talking about the need to inculcate a "zest for living" and a "zeal for learning" in the young? Why should a state school in southern Finland and a church school in south-west Korea have almost simultaneously decided to double the length of individual lessons and provide more time for group work and discussion? A snapshot study of this kind cannot fully explain such coincidences. But it can at least record how education thinking is changing and discuss some of the consequences.

Our search for ways in which children and young people can be motivated to become lifelong learners took us to not only the education ministries of eight countries but a total of 24 secondary schools and youth projects. We had asked each of the member countries involved to direct us to three examples of good practice that were:

- *Effective* in raising the motivation of students in secondary schools or immediate post-school settings, ideally with tangible outcomes.

- *Ambitious* and likely to be of interest to policy-makers and practitioners in different countries.

- *Innovative* in terms of *i*) curricula, assessment, qualifications *ii*) reorganisation of teaching and learning *iii*) partnerships involving education and other sectors.

- *Established* rather than just beginning, and likely to be sustainable over the medium-term given adequate support.

We said we were less interested in solitary examples of a good school or a motivating teacher and emphasised that the nominated projects should not only aim to hold students longer in school but really generate enthusiasm and motivation for learning. It was also made clear that our study would not focus simply on the needs of at-risk students – we said that some of the chosen initiatives should be directed at those who were not particularly disadvantaged.

At this stage, we should perhaps acknowledge that although this study concentrates on secondary students we accept that it is imperative that positive attitudes towards learning are developed while children are still in primary school. That, however, is a counsel of perfection that does not help the teachers who are trying to cope with students who are already in secondary schools. In any case, as Chapter 2 has pointed out, the research evidence suggests that motivation may be a bigger issue for secondary schools. Younger children tend to see effort as a uniformly good thing whereas older students are often badly hurt by any failure that follows great effort. They are therefore more likely not to try at all in order to protect their sense of "self-worth".

We were also conscious from the start that this study was seeking to do something that was extremely ambitious – not only to establish what motivates children (a tortuously difficult problem for the reasons given in Chapter 2) but also to separate out the particular strategies that would ensure they retained their appetite for learning throughout their adult life.

We do not pretend that we have achieved that miracle. The definitive answer to that question – including the kind of cost-benefit analysis – could only be arrived at by means of a longitudinal study that would take a considerable number of years. Neither would we claim that all of the predominantly urban schools and projects that we visited matched the rigorous criteria that we had hoped to apply. But in the real world of the classroom or the centre for unemployed teenagers there are relatively few thoroughly authenticated "magic solutions". We did, however, discover many examples of good practice that appeared to be laying firm foundations for the "learning society". And we came to realise that these foundations are being put down in an unimaginably diverse range of educational settings: a bomb shelter beneath a municipal swimming pool in Finland, a chicken shed in Korea, a fast-food restaurant in Japan, a clutch of converted farm buildings in Norway, a media centre in Denmark, an Icelandic college of vocational education just below the Arctic circle, an Internet café in Ireland and a local Chamber of Commerce in England.

But, ultimately, it was not the differences but the commonalities that became increasingly apparent as we compared notes, impressions and evaluation findings collected during our visits. It is true that national education systems remain as different and distinct as their languages and customs – even in relatively homogeneous regions of the world such as Scandinavia. But as Chapter 3 has indicated there is perhaps a surprising degree of similarity in government policy approaches to the motivation of school students and the promotion of lifelong learning. Equally, in the schools and youth projects we found much the same concerns being expressed in all eight countries and a relatively strong consensus on how children could be motivated to become lifelong learners.

In compiling the following digest of what we learned at the 24 study sites we decided it would be most helpful to pose virtually the same questions as were asked in Chapter 2. It would then be possible to cross-check to see whether our study confirms or contradicts some of the previous research into motivation. As will become apparent, the research findings largely tallied with the good practice that we witnessed. But we believe that this study provides some significant new insights, too, and raises a number of policy issues that will be discussed at the end of this chapter.

What was being done to motivate disaffected and disadvantaged students

Most of the education officials and teachers we met were unfamiliar with the American research into motivating difficult-to-reach students but they evidently shared the same philosophy as McCombs and Pope, two of the researchers quoted in Chapter 2. "Individuals are naturally motivated to learn when they do not have to fear failure, when they perceive what they are learning as being personally meaningful and relevant and when they are in respectful and supportive relationships with teachers."

As one of the Norwegian education professionals who contributed to this study said, many students are "mesmerised" by previous experiences of failure. Time and again the teachers of disaffected and disadvantaged students told us that their first – and key – task was to restore children's self-esteem and convince them that they did have the ability to learn.

The records of achievement that enable young people to register the progress they are making are one important method of achieving this goal that has been adopted by several of the schools visited. And as the Icelandic chapter illustrates, computer-based schemes that enable students to continue working until they get the right answers can also help to reassure those who may have lost confidence in their learning abilities.

But as McCombs and Pope say, it is not enough to reassure students that they can learn. The schools and youth projects we visited realised that they also had to offer students meaningful learning experiences. The Irish YOUTHREACH scheme neatly achieves both these aims by enabling unemployed 15 to 18-year-olds to master computer skills and then share them with members of the public. It also provides youngsters in the poorest areas with a safe, caring environment – something that US research has identified as essential in schemes of this kind.

51

In Reykjavik's Borgarholt School, maths lessons are being made more meaningful through practical exercises such as map reading. And in Kjelle School in Norway socially disadvantaged students are being offered specially-adapted courses in Health and Food Processing, Woodworking, Engineering and other subjects that should be highly relevant to their adult life. However, Vipunen school in East Finland goes one step further. Not only does it provide a wide range of practical skills training, it also permits students to learn "on the job" rather than in classrooms. Some students get their "theory lessons" under a vehicle bonnet in the school's car repair workshop. Others are allowed to complete their course on the premises of a local employer, though they remain under the school's supervision.

The school has realised that it has to be highly flexible if it is not only to hold on to – but motivate – some of its most troubled teenagers. Some students are therefore even allowed to start and finish at a later time. But the principal is not apologetic about her school's extreme flexibility, arguing that every student has to be treated as an individual. The hunt for the best solution is, for her, like searching for a hidden door. "When we find it we look for the key rather than try to kick it open", she said. As indicated in Chapter 3, virtually all the schools for disadvantaged students that we visited believed that individualised learning experiences were essential.

This was true of Japan and Korea, too, even though their education systems are not noted for their individual approaches. In Shinjuku Yamabuki school in Tokyo, a shift system allows former truants and drop-outs to attend on a day and time convenient to them. In Korea, a school for drop-outs run by a Buddhist sect is also providing far more choice and freedom than they ever experienced in mainstream schools. Not only can they choose between eight or nine physical education options, they can wear their hair as they like and go barefoot if they want to. The policy at this school, and several others, was to loosen the reins, without letting go entirely.

Schools in Iceland and Finland were also prepared to suspend the timetable for a week in order to concentrate on one subject if that would enable students to feel comfortable with a topic or master the knowledge that was needed to improve their chances of doing well in a test. However, there seems to be a consensus that students with problems need *physical space* as well as time. Classes catering for their special needs were always smaller than average – containing as few as six students in Finland and no more that 30 in Korea. Perhaps it was no coincidence either that the production school in Denmark, Kjelle School in Norway and Young-San Sung-Ji High School in Korea all had farm settings. The Korean school used the farm to teach self-sufficiency, and this was singled out as important in other schools, such as Kjelle, too.

The Danish, Norwegian, Korean and Finnish schools catering for the most challenging students also offered dormitory accommodation. This not only allowed some students to get away from volatile family relationships, it was another means of bonding with other students and the staff. The use of the word "staff" rather than "teachers" is deliberate. Although it was customary for such students to have one trusted and caring adult they could turn to for advice and help it was not necessarily a teacher. The Scandinavian schools all had a full panoply of welfare staff – social workers, education counsellors, dormitory supervisors and nurses.

This back-up was less evident in the other four countries. However, the English training scheme for curriculum support assistants who help children with special needs was another reminder of how non-teaching staff can also help to motivate students. And in Kuninkaanhaka school in west Finland even the canteen staff were expected to act as caring role models. The oft-quoted African proverb, "It takes a whole village to raise a child", is never more apposite than when talking about disadvantaged and potentially disaffected students.

How teaching approaches and school organisation can affect motivation levels

All the teachers we interviewed seemed to expect their students to learn. That may seem a trite statement, but unfortunately, as Chapters 1 and 2 pointed out, there is ample evidence that some teachers categorise students as good or bad and do not consider it their responsibility to try to change their attitudes towards learning. In one of the English schools where attainment levels had been low, teachers not only tried to restore children's self-confidence, they let it be known that higher standards were expected. They apparently got the desired response.

But, of course, demanding higher standards and greater motivation is pointless unless the ground is prepared for change. A more individualised approach to the curriculum had been adopted in most of the study sites we visited, not only those catering for disadvantaged students. Wherever we went we heard that teachers are stepping back and encouraging children to become autonomous learners. Lecture time is being reduced and more time is being given over to individual and group work, problem-solving exercises and discussion. As children become more used to working on their own or in groups rather than waiting for directions it appears to become easier for the teacher to find time to stimulate a child who may be less interested in the set exercises.

The Korean church school included in this study had created more timetable space for group activity and discussion by reducing the time that students spend copying material from the blackboard. In some countries the group work was taking the form of simulation exercises. In Sandefjord school in Norway, for example, students were "manufacturing" soap from fish oil and were even using new technology to communicate with students in a "factory" in Germany. At another Norwegian school, Nesodden, students were also being given a realistic – and apparently motivating – taste of adult life by using Powerpoint demonstrations to report their project findings. The importance of new technology can sometimes be overstated but these were by no means the only examples of how students' learning experiences could be extended through ICT. In Mankkaa school in Finland, for example staff have found that the Internet has awakened girls' interest in computers because it enables them to communicate rather than merely play games.

But computers do more than enrich a curriculum, of course. They can enable schools to transform the whole process of teaching and learning. The College of Vocational Training in Akureyri, Iceland, has established a distance learning course for students who cannot attend normal classes, either because of disability family or work commitments, or the fact that they live in remote areas. These students are able to follow the school's regular curriculum and take the same examinations under identical conditions as the mainstream students. The students appreciate the freedom to work when they want to, and the promise of "next day" feedback helps to ensure that their motivation levels are maintained.

Finnish upper-secondary students are also being given more say over what, where and when they study. They can, in theory, spend part of the week at a traditional academic school and the remainder in a vocational school. In practice, timetabling and transport problems still often thwart this aim. However, Finnish students can suspend their studies for a few weeks or months in order to pursue an interest or train for a sports competition. Such freedom is now becoming more common because many schools in both the East and West are no longer allotting upper-secondary students to year groups. This becomes possible when graduation is dependent on the accumulation of a specific number of credits or points rather than the completion of a set period of study. This can lead to complex timetabling arrangements and can sometimes prove costly in staffing terms but the statistical and anecdotal evidence we collected suggested that it is a relatively reliable way of motivating older students.

The influence of parents

As we indicated earlier, this study was primarily designed to examine how schools and out-of-school centres – rather than parents – can affect children's motivation. It was not feasible to carry out our own separate study of how parents in eight countries might be influencing their children's views on education. But if readiness to make financial contributions is the best gauge of how seriously parents regard their children's education then there is little doubt that the Japanese and Koreans are in a different league from parents in the other six countries. The amount that Koreans spend on private tutors for their children is, on average, more than half what the government invests in state education.

But, of course, parents in European countries take education very seriously too. In Finland, for example, almost half the adult population (aged 18 to 64) is said to take part in some form of education or training every year. It was also noticeable that wherever we went in Finland, parents' representatives were introduced as key partners who not only had a say in how schools were run but the curriculum they offered. However, schools and municipalities in both the East and the West admitted that they were worried by the number of "latchkey" children who were receiving inadequate support from their parents. In Japan, family relationships were said to be deteriorating because parents were working longer hours and more fathers were being obliged to work far from home.

Extrinsic motivation

This study suggests that extrinsic rewards – though often decried – can motivate some students in certain circumstances. Not only the very able who are competing for the glittering academic prizes but the average and less able teenagers, too. In Korea, vocational high school students were being coaxed to work hard by a partnership arrangement with junior colleges that enhanced their chances of winning places at the two-year higher education institutions. But this scheme also holds out the promise of a more stimulating curriculum that may generate more intrinsic interest in the subjects studied.

Unemployed teenagers in Ireland's YOUTHREACH programme clearly appreciated the public recognition they had received by producing a film that was shown on national television and reaching the final of a local enterprise competition. The new qualification for less academic Irish students, the Leaving Certificate Applied, also appeared to be an effective "carrot". The students we met did not have any sense of failure for not having attempted the traditional Leaving Certificate programme but rather a sense of achievement for tackling the new course.

An even more obvious extrinsic reward – money – was also helping to maintain some students' motivation levels in Finland. The hairdressers and woodworkers of Vipunen evidently felt that the opportunity to earn cash during the summer by working for one of the school's commercial enterprises was a strong reason to continue their courses. But they were not motivated by money alone and were clearly proud of the skills they had acquired.

Discussion

Some might say that what we witnessed were not initiatives designed to motivate students to become lifelong learners but attempts to "condition" them for working life in the 21st century. It is generally acknowledged that during the 19th century and for much of the 20th, schools resembled the factories that their students would one day work in. Teachers were overseers, school bells were the factory whistle. Now, as that method of production is outdated, schools are adapting to suit employers' needs. Hence the emphasis on problem-solving, group work, individual projects, Powerpoint presentations, creativity and information communication technology (ICT). Even the repeated references to the need for self-sufficiency can be regarded in this light. Some will see it as tacit acknowledgement that the days of full employment are permanently over.

But it is even more likely that the schools were responding to another reality – that they are now having to cope with a very different "clientele" than in the past. As young people are now spending more years in school it would not have been possible to go on offering them the same educational diet as was offered to under-15s, or the most academic 15 to 18-year-olds, a generation ago. Something had to give – especially as ICT is providing many more methods of knowledge transmission and human communication.

This tension is particularly evident in Korea where societal and economic change have been especially rapid, and traditional and modern educational approaches are co-existing uneasily. It is often said that cultures cannot be uprooted and replanted in another country. But a youth culture that is created and sustained by the global media is perhaps one of the exceptions to that rule. In Helsinki and Seoul young people were wearing the same baseball caps, listening to the same music and wearing identical sports gear. It therefore seems improbable that the kind of systemic student-centred education reforms described in the Korean chapter can be resisted much longer. Nevertheless, it will be a long time – if ever – before a universal curriculum and teaching strategies are adopted. The schools of the East and West remain very different, despite their occasional, freakish similarities.

It is therefore very difficult to say whether the schemes and teaching strategies that are specific to certain countries could be transferred from the Occident to the Orient, or *vice-versa*. It is even hard to point to the good practice that should be adopted by countries in the same regions. OECD member governments and their municipalities, head teachers and teachers will be the best judges of that as they have an intimate knowledge of their own systems and practices.

In any case, it could be argued that none of these initiatives will – on their own – guarantee that lifelong learning habits are embedded in the young. Children and adults need to be more than motivated if they are to become lifelong learners. They also need to be curious and persistent. Some of the statistics and official testimonies that are set out in the country chapters suggest that many of the young people we encountered will develop all of these traits. But such evidence can never tell the whole story. The individual anecdotes collected during a study of this kind can also be highly revealing. Two, in particular, highlight what we consider to be fundamental truths that must be borne in mind whenever the subject of student motivation is discussed. Both came out of the Finnish study but, in this instance, the country is irrelevant as the conversations could have taken place in any of the other seven countries. What these two anecdotes underline is that attitudes towards learning are not only determined by schools, important though they are.

At one lower-secondary school a special needs teacher said that some of her most troubled students could not settle down to work in the morning until they had had an opportunity to talk about their personal and family problems. At another school in an area of Eastern Finland that suffers from high unemployment a former student was brought in to air his sardonic views on the vocational course he had just completed. "I'm glad I did the course... if I hadn't done it I would not have qualified for unemployment pay."

The first anecdote confirms that children's interest in schoolwork cannot be kindled if their personal lives are clouded by domestic strife, poverty or crime. The second reminds us that the task of engaging less able students becomes infinitely harder if they suspect that there will be no jobs for them when they leave school – no matter how hard they work.

Members of the Board who discussed this study at their November 1999 meeting stressed that the following factors can also undermine efforts to promote student motivation for lifelong learning: the policy of forcing lower achievers to repeat grades; the short-sightedness of some employers who encourage young people to leave school prematurely – particularly where the economy is booming – and then provide them with little or no education and training opportunities; education systems' general tendency to expend too much effort on sorting and grading students rather than developing their abilities and improving their attitudes towards learning; and schools' failure to harness the power of the youth culture that often seems far more relevant to teenagers than a curriculum dictated by adults. The importance of some reflection on policy process and raising the motivation level of policy-makers themselves was also underlined.

None of these problems is new and none will be solved easily, if at all. Nevertheless, there is much in the following country chapters to make us optimistic that a great deal can be achieved in even an imperfect world.

Key Policy Considerations

Lifelong learning: Our study shows that governments appear to have placed lifelong learning at the centre of their educational policy-making. They have achieved a consensus on some key issues in the lifelong learning agenda, including school organisation, curricula, and support services. Now it is crucial to clarify the roles of education institutions and other stakeholders, such as communities, parents and employers. Related issues such as accountability, financing and resource allocation also need to be carefully considered.

Issues for higher education: Competition for entry to higher education has caused some governments to express concern about the implications of intensive examination preparation. Yet, changing the traditional exams system was not high on the agendas. Some countries have introduced new learning assessment tools such as records of achievement. But such tools will have only limited value if higher education institutions or employers do not acknowledge them.

Teachers: Like their students, teachers need incentives to change. They, too, must be motivated to take on an agenda for lifelong learning. In most countries, training to equip teachers for innovation appears to be insufficient. The goal of developing a lifelong learning culture is unlikely to be achieved if teachers and school managements are inadequately prepared for such a revolutionary change.

Gender issues: These may be receiving insufficient attention. In some countries, there are marked gender differences in young people's post-secondary education and career pathways. It is most likely that these disparities affect their level of motivation. Yet government policies seem to give little attention to this issue. Although boys are often harder to motivate and girls lack motivation in specific subject areas, these problems are not being addressed fully either.

The importance of students' perception and input: During our visits, students' perceptions and experiences were quite revealing. Reflecting their views on policies and programmes is essential as one of lifelong learning's key features, a learner-centred approach, places emphasis on students' initiative and "ownership" in learning. The days when they were merely passive recipients of knowledge are over.

Above-average students: Initiatives aimed at raising student motivation appear to be focused on the disadvantaged and disaffected. This is not only sensible but commendable. However, it would be wrong to exclude academically successful children from the discussion about motivation and lifelong learning. A student who has been drilled to perform well within the conventional educational system may not be equipped for lifelong learning.

Research relevant to policy priorities: If policy development is to be properly informed, relevant research is essential. In some countries there was a surprising absence of formal evaluation studies on innovative projects. Longitudinal research on the factors that promote lifelong learning would be particularly helpful. More research into how motivation levels are affected by a young person's developmental stage and different learning and career pathways could also be extremely useful.

Part II
COUNTRY CASE STUDIES

DENMARK

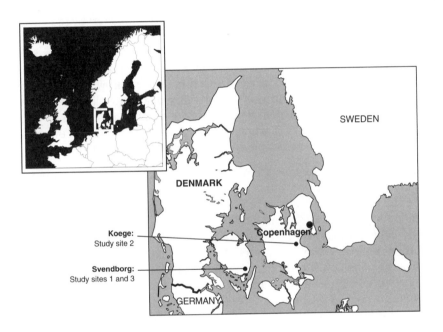

Land area in square kilometers: 43 000.

Total population (1998): 5 301 000.

Youth population – under 15 years (1998):
  – 959 481,
  – percentage of total population: 18.1%.

Youth unemployment (1998):
  – 15-24 year-olds: 7.2%.

Percentage of 18-year-olds in education (1998): 74%.

Per capita GDP (1997 prices): 25 514 USD.

Birth rate per 1 000 population (1996): 12.9.

Sources: *Labour Force Statistics: 1979-1998,* OECD, Paris; *Annual National Accounts, Main Aggregates, Volume 1, 1999,* OECD, Paris; *Education at a Glance,* OECD Database 1999, Paris.

Country context

Education: Human resources have long been considered Denmark's main asset and education is seen as an important factor in the country's economic success. "It (education) is a way of life among the Danes, a rarely questioned, deeply held value."* Education is compulsory from the age of 7, but nearly all children attend at least one year of pre-school classes. The municipal *folkeskole* provides compulsory education for nine years, plus an optional tenth year, which was introduced in the mid-1970s and is now completed by the majority of students. After leaving the *folkeskole* at the age of 15 or 16, 95 per cent of young Danes proceed to some form of "youth education". Just over 50 per cent go into general upper secondary education, more than 40 per cent enter vocational education and most of the remainder follow individual programmes designed for those who are not willing or able to follow the two main streams. Almost three in four 18-year-olds are enrolled in secondary education, compared to an OECD average of 51 per cent (1996 figures). But no less than 84 per cent of young people complete some kind of youth education.

Economy: In a few decades, Denmark has transformed itself from a predominantly agricultural society into an advanced post-industrial economy. Agriculture still accounts for nearly 40 per cent of exports but employs less than 5 per cent of the workforce. The emphasis has been switching to the production of high technology goods that meet exacting standards. A very substantial proportion of these goods is exported. Denmark's GDP per capita is one of the highest among OECD countries (US$32 000 in 1997), and private investment, disposable incomes and consumption have all increased rapidly in recent years. The country's satisfactory growth rates, together with structural reforms, have resulted in a substantial decline in unemployment, from 12 per cent in 1993 to just under 6 per cent in 1999, and unemployment among 15 to 24-year-olds is now relatively low. The percentage of women in the workforce is high, but has been declining lately. In the labour market, a clear distinction is made between skilled and unskilled workers, which may be one of the motivations for young people to obtain qualifications.

---

*   In addition to the background report prepared by the Danish authorities for this study, two recent OECD reports on the transition from initial education to working life have been used here. They provide a comprehensive description of the system and a stimulating analysis of the problems which are often closely related to student motivation issues. See *Thematic Review of the Transition from Initial Education to Working Life. The Danish Country Report*, Ministry of Education, June 1998; "Country note: Denmark", OECD, March 1999.

Student motivation issues

Denmark's demographic and economic background should be borne in mind when looking at the problem of student motivation for lifelong learning. Falling birth rates have meant that fewer young people have been completing their secondary education and entering the labour market (the birth rate is just beginning to rise again). This has two effects that are relevant to this study. First, since the schools are financed on a per-capita basis, they are competing to attract more students. As many schools are small, recruitment is often a matter of survival.

The second implication is that employers are increasingly looking for skilled labour, especially in sectors and occupations that are considered unattractive. As a result, there is pressure from both the education sector and from industry to encourage young people to continue their studies and to acquire a qualification. This is reinforced by legislation which stipulates that unemployment pay should cease after a limited period if a young person does not accept either the jobs offered to them, or additional training.

But the most important factor to be considered with regard to motivation is probably the Danes' tradition of valuing education and the general belief that a democratic society cannot accept exclusion. In addition, with an economy that is technologically advanced and is competitive largely thanks to its skilled labour force, the requirements for not being left behind are comparatively higher than in other countries.

While intake into upper secondary education is clearly above the OECD average, the retention rate is not seen as satisfactory, particularly in comparison with other Nordic countries. As a result of substantial drop-outs, particularly in the vocational stream, approximately 84 per cent of a cohort complete a youth education. The Ministry of Education now recognises that vocational education is insufficiently attractive and the drop-out rates are too high.

A 1998 Danish government report[1] identified low skill acquisition as an important problem, and suggested this was linked to inadequate motivation and incentives to complete upper secondary education and pursue higher-level studies. This critical view contrasts sharply with the very positive picture usually found in the national and international literature (including the OECD's 1999 report on the transition from school to work). It may be because one of the contributors to the report was the Ministry of Finance, which has been accused of putting more

---

1. Ministries of Education, Research Labour, Business, Finance, Economic Affairs and the Prime Minister's Office, *Kvalitet i uddannelsessystemet.*

emphasis on the cost and effectiveness of the system than on its educational and social value.

The issue of drop-outs has received much attention from researchers and policy-makers. A research project called "Education for All", undertaken in the mid 1990s, found, unsurprisingly, that social background has an important impact on participation in youth education. But it also discovered that youngsters who had succeeded in lower secondary school went on to some form of further education even when they came from low-income and poorly-educated families. This suggests that the quality of teaching in primary and lower secondary education should be a focus of further studies.

The "Education for All" research found that many girls with poor academic skills drop out of vocational training and many of them complain that the course had too little practical content. Some students criticise the quality and organisation of the teaching: almost one-third of those who drop out say that teachers are not good enough. Students would prefer more varied forms of teaching that allow them to play a more active role. They would also like to have more attention paid to their opinions. The study also established that youngsters attach great importance to personal and social development: more than one quarter of them gave poor social climate as the reason for dropping out. This concern was quite obvious when discussions were held with students during the visit.

It should be underlined that a substantial proportion of the apparent drop-outs are, in fact, moving from one type of education to another (especially from the gymnasium to vocational schools and, to some extent, from vocational schools to individual programmes). Moving around and taking much time to complete an education seems to be a Danish trait that is encouraged by the diversity of the system and by its comparatively high degree of flexibility. It may be partly justified by the fact that most young people are working part-time while studying – which suggests that they are not wasting their time.

The complexity of the education system and the diversity of pathways make guidance and counselling particularly important. They are fairly well developed in Denmark, but have come under criticism. Several institutions and types of staff are involved and the quality of provision and the level of staff training vary greatly. Many counsellors are not sufficiently trained in labour-market issues and the system does not seem to pay enough attention to the most vulnerable groups.

Immigration is a rather recent phenomenon in Denmark and the proportion of young people coming from countries such as Turkey, Pakistan and the former Yugoslavia is still comparatively small. Some of them seem highly motivated to study and to do well at school. But many have a language handicap and face problems of cultural and social integration. It may be more difficult for them to find their ways in a complex system.

Main policy approaches

Various educational policies have been developed to meet these challenges. Since 1996, all young people under the age of 25 who have neither an occupational qualification nor one that allows them to enter tertiary education have been obliged to – or had the right to – participate in education for at least 18 months. In November 1998, a "Development Programme for Youth Education" was introduced in the Danish parliament. It stated that 95 per cent of young people should complete a full youth education and 50 per cent should complete further education.

In order to reach these targets, two sets of measures are being implemented, which are in line with the educational policies that the Danish government has pursued for several decades. They aim to:

- Further improve the quality, efficiency and attractiveness of mainstream upper secondary education.
- Offer alternative opportunities or safety nets for those who are not willing or able to stay in the mainstream.

Improvement in general and vocational education

The "Education for All" research stimulated discussions at the national level on student participation and retention and helped to reduce drop-out rates. More recently, government initiatives such as Reform-2000 of the vocational and education and training system[2] have addressed the same issues. It proposes that:

- Vocational education should become more attractive and have higher status.
- Students should be able to switch programmes.
- Vocational programmes should offer more possibilities of proceeding to higher levels of study.
- The curriculum should be more focused on preparation for lifelong education.

These objectives would require:

- More individual pathways.
- A new approach to teaching and learning: the role of teachers would be modified, with more teamwork, and more emphasis on guidance and individual coaching of students.
- A more inviting college culture.

---

2. On the basis of the paper prepared by: Finn Christensen, *The Important and Innovative Features of the Reform -2000 of the Danish VET System*, Ministry of Education, January 1999.

- More options for low-achievers such as a certificate for specific vocational skills that would be on a lower level than the existing qualifications for skilled workers.

The national "Development programme" is not limited to vocational education. It aims to make the entire youth education system broader and more coherent by "building bridges" between different sectors of education. Other goals include: easing the transition from lower to upper secondary education; promoting more self-directed student activities; developing educational and vocational guidance; and improving the quality of education and level of student performance.

Many local initiatives could also have a significant impact. Some are seeking to establish a closer relationship between schools and parents and to encourage recent immigrants to send their children to the kindergarten. Local authorities are also concerned with the other end of the age range as they have a legal duty to make sure that school-leavers either find a job, get some training or go back for more education.

Alternative youth education programmes

In 1993, a new programme of basic vocational education and training was established to meet the needs of less academically-minded young people. As it is administered by local authorities, its development has been uneven. The general reluctance to promote training activities that do not lead to a recognised qualification has been a further hindrance.

The open youth education programme is more innovative. It is intended for young people who are not attracted by more traditional programmes of youth education but is also available to adults. Students compose their own programme from a variety of courses with the help of an authorised guidance counsellor, and they can include study visits abroad. During the programme, which lasts at least two years, students are connected to a state-recognised institution and are supported by a counsellor.

One survey indicated that only 30 per cent of the participants would have pursued another form of education if this opportunity had not been available. But only 2 per cent of young people take part in the programme and it is unlikely to be extended.

The *production schools* represent the third alternative programme of youth education. Created in 1980 by the Ministry of Education to combat youth unemployment, there are now 105 of these schools. They have a duty to "provide integrated learning and production programmes for young people under 25 years of age with no prior post-compulsory education [...] to strengthen personal growth in participants and enhance their opportunities in the education system and their employability".

Production schools are also designed to meet local needs and they differ widely, depending on their origin and inspiration. Some have been influenced by the people's enlightenment tradition of Grundtvig, the philosopher and educationist who founded the Folk High School. Others are based on the concept of learning by doing, and a third group has grown out of various municipal projects for unemployed people.

As they are not part of the formal school system, production schools do not require participants to enrol for fixed periods. Initially, they catered solely for unemployed youth, but this limitation was lifted in 1996.

In addition to these main programmes, five cities have residential schools offering labour-market courses for marginalised groups. The municipalities also run training programmes for young people who have been out of work for a prolonged period, usually at least three months.

"The complexity of the education system and the diversity of the pathways make guidance and counselling particularly important."

"The objectives are to stimulate interaction and to encourage the participants to express themselves and to learn to respect other people."

STUDY SITES

Case study No. 1

Institution:	**Produktionshojskolen**
Location:	**Svendborg, Funen Island**
Starting date:	1984

Svendborg is one of Denmark's 105 production schools but it aims to do more than teach vocational skills. Its real goal is to produce young adults who are ready for life.

This is one of the most important production schools in the country. It was established in an old farm that was renovated and enlarged by the students themselves. The management seems to enjoy a fair amount of autonomy, under the responsibility of a board, which includes representatives from employers, trade unions and the municipality. Most of the financing, which is only for those aged 16 to 25 is provided by the Ministry of Education. Less than 10 per cent comes from the municipality and sales of products and services.

Provided they attend regularly, the participants receive weekly unemploy ment benefits of DKK 440 (US$62) up to the age of 18 and DKK 1 070 afterwards i they are not living with their parents. The school has 47 employees anc 230 students (called "participants") at a time. They come from 11 local communi ties and stay from two months to two years – but the average is about eigh months. Most participants have stayed in school until grade 9 or 10, but have ther failed or dropped out. The main objective is therefore to motivate them to study again, rather than to prepare them for a job.

The emphasis is put on integrated learning and on a student-centred approach. The day usually starts with an informal group meeting, where any topic may be discussed. The objectives are to stimulate interaction and to encourage the participants to express themselves and to learn to respect other people. The daily, communal lunches for students and staff are accompanied by readings stories and songs.

The only set studies are in Danish language and maths, which are taught twice a week for two hours by outside teachers to those participants who wish to attend. Participants can also follow five or six-week courses that have been specially designed for them at local vocational schools where they are able to use more sophisticated equipment. Some participants may spend a few weeks in a firm with constant support and supervision by the school.

The school's 19 departments offer a range of activities that take account of the young people's needs and those of the market. Normally, the participant stays in one department, but it is also possible to move between departments. Most of the activities are based on what could motivate the young people. They include:

- *Auto-mechanics*: the participants assemble karts, or parts of an old car, or do simple repairs for an outside client.

- *Theatre and music practice*: this is primarily for self-development and expression but the music group also performs outside the school.

- *Kitchen*: the participants prepare food, including bread and pastry, for the whole school.

Three counsellors are attached full-time to several departments. They visit each of them every week and have discussions with the group on social behaviour and on any problem that may arise. They have regular individual contacts with all participants, discuss their plans and try to help them to solve their educational and personal problems. Participants have a logbook in which they and the coun- sellors can record their activities and progress. Counsellors are also responsible for organising work-experience placements.

One counsellor helps participants who have serious problems concerning housing, drugs or alcoholism. A house is available for those who have nowhere to live and the school maintains close contact with social services officials.

The media centre is particularly impressive. It is located in separate and very pleasant premises in town, and has its own cafeteria. It had 95 participants at the time of the visit and admits 150 a year. It houses nine of the school's departments, in such areas as graphics, computer maintenance, local radio broadcasting, digital editing of TV programmes, journalism, and designing home-pages for the Internet. The centre owns no fewer than 100 computers and has the most up-to-date technology. The initial equipment was provided by the Ministry of Education, but some of the later purchases have been funded by the sales of products and services.

It is surprising to see the participants doing jobs that look very professional and complex, although they are said to have a low level of education. The work they do looks so exciting and the environment is so pleasant that an outsider would expect that youngsters might prefer to work there rather than study in a regular school. In fact, almost all candidates are accepted and the waiting list is relatively short. This is because production schools do not offer a formal qualification and have traditionally been seen to cater for the least talented youngsters.

In the centre, as in the rest of the production school, it was strongly emphasised that the objective is not to prepare participants for a job, but to help them to develop their personality and an awareness of what they want to do. Returning to school for more education is the goal. There are no statistics on what happens to participants after they leave, but apparently the majority do go back for some kind of education. Even the practical competence they can acquire in the media sector is not sufficient to make them very attractive for employers, who can find other candidates with more education.

Case study No. 2

Institution:	**KoegeHandelsskole**
Location:	**Koege, Zealand Island**
Starting date:	**1996**

The realisation that weaker students in the vocational stream were not thriving has prompted this upper secondary school to rip up the timetable and start again.

This school provides vocational courses and upper secondary education with a vocational emphasis to the equivalent of 1 500 full-time students. The school is largely autonomous and is governed by an executive committee including representatives of business and unions. But the Ministry of Education is the main

71

source of financing. It funds the school on a per-capita basis (the so-called "taxi meter" system), which is an incentive to recruit more students. Additional income is produced by courses for adults and some consultancy work.

The school has a charismatic principal and is regarded as one of the best in the country. Its premises are spacious and well-designed and it is generously equipped with modern computers. In 1996, the school asked the government for additional resources to offer new activities to weaker students in the vocational stream. The ministry agreed to the request on condition that an innovative project was developed.

As a result, the vocational stream students no longer need to attend traditional classes. New methods of teaching have been introduced and a closer relationship between the students and the teacher has been established. The students are given options and select what they want to study, after consultations with their tutor. There is a tutor for each team of 10 to 12 students. Each team covers a full range of subjects and is responsible for the planning of all activities. Students divide their time between work of their choice and team activities. There is a lot of emphasis on activities which may contribute to the development of the personality and of socialisation. A logbook will be introduced to monitor the progress of each student.

Studies take place with members of other teams. They may involve courses on a given subject, case studies, project work or simulation exercises (for example, simulation of an office environment for students of commerce).

Surveys have shown that teachers are generally positive about the new system. Typical comments are: "The job is more interesting, they know the students better, they are more open to each other, the workplace is more democratic and some of them like the longer teaching periods that the system involves." However, teachers also have some negative comments: "There is too much work, too little time for counselling, uncertainty as to who has learnt what – and when [...] it is difficult to know where you are in the process – and to see the aim clearly [...] also difficult to take over from one teacher to another during a course."

Discussions were held during the visit with a group of teachers who were comparatively young and appear particularly motivated. They consider themselves "developers" rather than teachers and none would like to return to the old system. "It is much more fun like this", one said. Teaching is now far more inter-disciplinary and teachers sometimes have to develop courses and presentations about a subject that is entirely new to them. But some of their colleagues had been unable to adapt to the new system and had asked for a transfer into the regular stream.

A survey of students also drew mixed responses. Two of the positive comments were: "The daily work seems more meaningful and less boring [...] it is easier to make friends." But some felt the system could be chaotic and there was some uncertainty as to whether they were learning enough. The students who were interviewed during the visit were often shy and reluctant to draw comparisons with other schools. However, the teachers believe that the students would not like to move back to the traditional school.

Case study No. 3

Institution:	HF-Sofart
Location:	Svendborg, Funen Island
Starting date:	August 1998

The designers of a new course in shipping and marine engineering hope that the prospect of work-experience at sea will encourage less academic teenagers to prolong their general education.

As young people in Denmark are no longer willing to accept the constraints that maritime occupations have always entailed, there is now an acute shortage of qualified personnel and specialised schools are under-utilised. Employers would also like to recruit staff with a better general education.

Principals of several maritime schools and of a high school have therefore organised, on their own initiative, a three-year sandwich course leading to a new hybrid qualification. Recruitment takes place after the completion of lower secondary school (grade 9 or 10). Education and training periods alternate between:

- A gymnasium.
- Two technical colleges specialising in navigation and in marine engineering.
- A pre-sea private (Christian) school, which provides basic and practical training.

Two years are spent in the gymnasium and six months in each of the technical schools. A first group of 23 students (all boys) was recruited in August 1998.

At the time of the visit, they were in their seventh week in the gymnasium. Although following a different path from the other students, they were expected to undertake the same programme and to sit the same examination as the other vocationally-biased students. During their first months at the gymnasium, the behaviour of the shipping and marine engineering students was considered unsatisfactory, and teachers felt that they were weaker than the others in academic subjects. But it was hoped that they would catch up before the end of the course.

The students who were interviewed appeared to be self-confident and strongly motivated. They were well aware of the new opportunities offered to them and were keen to have some practical experience (the course allows them to go on board a ship for short periods). They were also aware that preparing for a

73

double qualification gives them more time to think about their future. Both aspects may attract more students to the course.

It is too early to assess how successful the course will be. But other schools in Jutland are taking an interest in the project, and a larger group of students, which included girls, was recruited for the course in August 1999.

* * *

Innovation and effectiveness

Having reviewed the main policies and the three projects which illustrate them, three questions arise:

- To what extent are they innovative and relevant to student motivation?
- Are they cost-effective?
- Are they replicable on a larger scale (which is related to the cost-effectiveness issue)?

Innovative and meaningful experiments

The extent to which the three projects are innovative could be argued, since they are clearly in line with established policies that have emphasised flexibility, individualisation, and student-centred approaches. However, they go one step further than has been usual in Denmark, and probably much further than schools in many other countries.

The emphasis on individual students, especially the weaker ones, is impressive. It is particularly remarkable that (at least in the first two projects), the objective is often not to prepare students for instrumental targets – not even for getting a job – but to develop their personality, their autonomy and their self-confidence. It is assumed that with more maturity, and in a pleasant environment, they will be more motivated for further studies, which in turn will prepare them for the world of work and its rising requirements.

The attention to the individual learner is also not limited to educational problems. These projects often have to deal with youngsters who have personal, family and social problems. Helping young people to overcome them is a prerequisite for motivation and success in academic work.

Individualisation seems to be a permanent concern of Danish policies, but these students are given an exceptional degree of freedom to decide what they want to do and how. This may well be motivating because studying in this way is more exciting. The emphasis on self-learning also lays the foundation for lifelong learning.

Other countries have combined general and vocational courses in order to prepare for a double qualification but it was new in Denmark and was indeed a recommendation of the OECD report on transition from initial education to working life. What sets the marine engineering initiative apart is the fact that it was achieved through a partnership of very different schools. It will be interesting to see whether the prospect of more practical activities and work experience does encourage less academically-minded youngsters to follow a longer course of studies that contains a substantial proportion of general education.

One striking feature of the Danish projects is the role played by local initiative in the conception (in two of the cases) and development of the innovation (all three). The school management, assisted by a board that represents a wide range of local interests, enjoys considerable freedom and the central administration is primarily there to provide support and resources rather than give directions. Teachers are also very involved in developing curricula and teaching methods

Another interesting aspect is that a single major innovation (individualisation, bridge-building and partnership; learning by doing) has generally entailed a complete set of new learning approaches. They imply a more learner-centred pedagogy, a changing role for teachers, and more work experience. In other words, one innovation opens the door to others – or maybe these are necessary for the sake of coherence.

A characteristic which is common to the three projects and which seems to be specific to Denmark, is the importance attached to the learning environment and the social context. All the sites visited were spacious, lavishly equipped and nicely decorated. This was generally seen as a way of showing respect for students, including the most underprivileged ones. It is also a way to make the school more attractive. Equally remarkable was the importance that students attached to social relationships in school. In Denmark, a friendly atmosphere and the organisation of social events contribute to the prestige and attractiveness of an educational institution.

Effectiveness

A few scattered indications were obtained about the cost of the three experiments:

- In the commercial school, the start-up cost, underwritten by the Ministry of Education, was rather high, but it is estimated that the recurring costs are not much higher than for traditional courses.

- The Svendborg course costs more than usual because it lasts three years rather than two.

- The annual cost per participant at the production school was estimated at DKK 80 000 (slightly more than US$10 000), which corresponds to DKK 63 per hour. This does not include the allowance given to the participants. The cost per student in the vocational schools would be slightly lower on average but much higher for a comparable type of training.

But cost-per-student figures have very little meaning. A more useful cost-benefit analysis would have to include the indirect benefits of the experiments. And considering the type of population concerned, one should consider the alternative cost, for the individual and society, of not attending an educational institution. This is not always measurable. There are, however, national statistics showing that about 40 per cent of the production school participants continue their education or training, 20 per cent get a job, and 15 per cent find a subsidised job.

There are some statistics relating to the commercial school that are also worth bearing in mind. First, at the final examination, the school's students had better-than-average marks. Second, the drop-out rate went down from 12 to 6 per cent. Some schools have a drop-out rate of 16 per cent.

Replicability

The issue of replicability may be addressed in different ways: Is it desirable? Is it feasible from a financial, institutional and social point of view? The answer to these questions differs according to the programme.

The extension of the individualisation experiment in the commercial school to all vocational programmes is apparently now an objective of the Ministry of Education, but there are no plans to extend it to the regular high school stream. It is recognised that the initial period of development and experimentation was very demanding for the teachers and required additional resources provided by the Ministry.

The extension of a partnership between a gymnasium and technical schools to prepare double qualifications for various occupational sectors seems unlikely. Some believe that as there is already a great deal of flexibility in the system, this type of extension is not necessary.

The production schools are in a rather paradoxical situation. On the one hand, it is generally recognised that they are successful. However, the sharp fall in unemployment, together with financial restrictions, have discouraged the Ministry of Education from financing any increase in student numbers. The sites visited did seem expensive but very high unit costs could also probably be observed in a number of small, and sometimes under-utilised, institutions.

Of course, the weight of traditions and cultures also has to be taken into account. It was interesting to observe that teachers do not react to the innovations in the same way. Teachers from vocational schools seem more traditional than those in the production schools, but probably less so than those of the gymnasium. The success of the innovations observed is due largely to the high motivation of a specific group of teachers – and to the charisma of some managers. Whether teachers in general will participate in the pedagogic revolution which involves shifting from a teaching (or teacher-centred) approach to a learning (or learner-centred) approach remains to be seen.

In any case, the educational challenges implied by the three projects should not be under estimated. Broadly speaking, the basic goal is to attract young people who are supposed to be less talented and to upgrade their level to normal standards, thanks to non-conventional methods. This will require a large-scale programme of in-service training.

Commentary

In a country such as Denmark where education is highly valued and broadly-based, where participation is high at all levels and where there is a long tradition of lifelong learning, one might have doubted whether there was any problem of student motivation. This brief review suggests that there is, but probably at a higher level and for a smaller group of young people than in most other countries. It is also evident that the problem is being addressed by national policies and by individual institutions, with an impressive level of resources and of dedication.

Denmark is a rich country, but it would not be sufficient if the national culture and traditions were not so concerned with education and with the disadvantaged population. Clearly, the Danes are managing to motivate some disadvantaged young people, at least in a number of institutions, but in view of their specific context, there may be limits to the transferability to other countries.

FINLAND

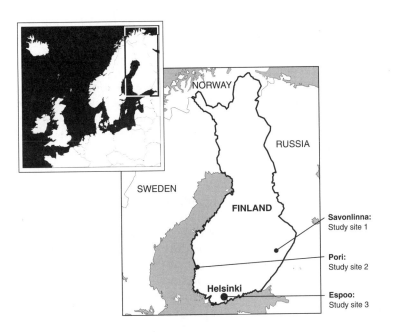

Land area in square kilometers: 338 000.

Total population (1998): 5 153 000.

Youth population – under 15 years (1998):
- 958 458,
- percentage of total population: 18.6%.

Youth unemployment (1998):
- 15-24 year-olds: 22.0%.

Percentage of 18-year-olds in education (1998): 85%.

Per capita GDP (1997 prices): 20 488 USD.

Birth rate per 1 000 population (1996): 11.8.

Sources: Labour Force Statistics: 1979-1998, OECD, Paris; *Annual National Accounts, Main Aggregates, Volume 1, 1999,* OECD, Paris; *Education at a Glance,* OECD Database 1999, Paris.

Country context

Education: The Finnish people place a high value on education, and opinion polls repeatedly show that almost 90 per cent of the public are satisfied with the education system. Its teachers are among the best-educated in Europe and international studies suggest that Finnish children are highly literate. The Finns are also considered to be excellent linguists even though they have had a reputation for being "silent in two languages" – the national languages of Finnish and Swedish. The lack of recent statistical evidence makes it harder to assess performance in maths and science but the government would like to see more students taking advanced courses in these subjects. The Ministry of Education's overall educational and training development goals are: high-quality education, equal opportunities and lifelong learning. Its expert agency, the National Board of Education, has produced a skeleton national curriculum, but as substantial powers are now invested in the 452 municipalities and individual schools the curriculum can be adapted to meet local needs and reflect parents' wishes. Finnish schools also face little or no accountability pressures in comparison with some other countries.

Economy: Over the past six years Finland has been recovering from the worst recession that any OECD country has experienced (OECD, 1998). The 1990-93 slump was partly caused by the collapse of the Soviet Union, which had a serious effect on the Finnish textile industry. GNP fell by 12 per cent and about 450 000 jobs vanished (Ministry of Labour, 1998), a massive loss for a country with a population of just over 5 million. Finland's growth rate is now well above the euro-area average and the unemployment rate dropped to 10 per cent last year. The jobs shortage remains a concern in the North and the East but Finland can now claim to be Europe's leading hi-tech economy. Its standard-bearer, Nokia, is the world's biggest manufacturer of mobile phones. Finland remains an archetypal Scandinavian welfare state and the Social Democrat-Conservative coalitions that have governed the country for the past five years have been criticised for cutting expenditure on welfare services. One in four Finns receives social security benefits but many see this as an essential part of a healthy social policy.

Student motivation issues

Finland's drop-out statistics and matriculation rates suggest that the country's teenagers are much more highly motivated than their contemporaries in most other nations. Only 200 15-year-olds out of 65 000 drop out before completing lower secondary school. More than 90 per cent of 17-year-olds are still in school and only 2-4 per cent of upper secondary school students fall by the wayside each year. Furthermore, the proportion of 18-year-old upper secondary school students passing the matriculation exam (about 94 per cent) is impressive. The vocational schools' drop-out rate is about 10 per cent but still below most other countries. And as Finland will have 29 polytechnics (AMKs) by the end of this year almost one in three vocational students is going on to higher education.

Truancy levels also appear to be low at all stages of education but there are no statistics to confirm this. There is, however, statistical evidence that the self-esteem of Finnish teenagers improved during the first half of the 1990s (Korpinen, 1990). In 1990, 60 per cent of students said they were "satisfied with themselves", but a 1995 study found that this figure had risen to 79 per cent (Tuomi, 1995). Finnish children also tend to rate their schools highly in terms of the opportunities to make friends. But some research (Linnakyla et al., 1996) indicates that only 50 per cent of Finnish students are happy at school. Finnish-speaking students often resent having to learn Swedish, which is the mother tongue of 6 per cent of the population, even though many career paths are closed to those who cannot speak the language. Science appears to be almost as unpopular and teacher-student relationships do not appear to be ideal either. One study (Kannas, 1995) found that Finnish boys and girls felt that they had much less encouragement from teachers to express opinions than young people in other countries – even those in neighbouring Scandinavian nations.

Perhaps predictably, Finnish boys appear to be generally harder to motivate than girls. They are said to enjoy some subjects – such as history – but more than 80 per cent of comprehensive school principals (Jakku-Sihvonen and Lindstrom, 1996) believe they present a greater challenge than girls. However, it is acknowledged that motivational problems cannot be wholly explained merely by reference to gender and curriculum. Half of the comprehensive school principals ascribed differences in students' motivation levels to cultural and social factors. Another study (Valijarvi and Tuomi, 1993) reported that upper-secondary students' motivation could be largely explained by the level of academic success they had experienced at comprehensive school.

The still substantial level of youth unemployment must also have an effect on motivation levels. The jobs shortage will inevitably cause some students to work harder and others to give up. Much the same can be said about the shortage of higher education places. Only 20 000 of the 50 000 applicants for university places are accepted each year. Some students consequently apply four years running before finding a place – an indication of the determination some young Finns show in their quest for higher education – but others must be left demotivated by the selection process. It is, however, clear that many of those who do not go on to higher education still retain some appetite for learning. The government considers that the average education level of the over-40s is still too low but it is heartened that no fewer than 1.6 million Finns take part in some form of adult or vocational education each year. There is a well-known saying in Finnish: *Oppia ika kaikki* (All life is learning) and many adults evidently take it literally.

Main policy approaches

The Finnish government has decided that education should be developed according to the principle of lifelong learning. The education system will therefore be *less institution-centred* in future and will encompass all forms of learning and environments, and all ages (partly because of concern over the large number of over-50-year-olds who are classified as long-term unemployed). Upper secondary distance learning courses for young people and adults who have a comprehensive school leaving certificate, or its equivalent, are an example of the new approaches being introduced to encourage lifelong learning. Students register with a local school but follow lessons broadcast by radio stations and can seek advice and counselling *via* the Internet.

The government also wants to raise the status of vocational education and *increase on-the-job learning*, believing that education and training that is perceived as more "relevant" will increase students' motivation. Since August 1999 all three-year vocational courses have had to offer six months' work experience to every student – an ambitious objective that may be difficult to achieve in areas of the country where there are relatively few employers. It is also hoped that apprenticeship training can continue to expand but this is another far-from-easy task as 99 per cent of Finnish firms have fewer than 50 employees.

Education policy-makers are also determined to *enhance student self-esteem* and enjoyment of school. Anti-bullying strategies are therefore being promoted. The government is also pursuing its predecessor's policy of eradicating the division between the lower comprehensive school (grades 1-6 for 7 to 12-year-olds) and the upper comprehensive sector (grades 7-9 for 13 to 15-year-olds). It wants teaching expertise to be shared by the two sectors – "A good teacher is a motivating teacher", one Board of Education official commented. But another objective of this policy is to see children more often grouped by ability rather than age. The government has already ensured that rigid age-grouping is disappearing from the upper secondary and vocational schools (for 16 to 18s). Students in the post-compulsory school sector now have much more freedom over what, when and where they study. Some see this as the most effective way of ensuring that the young are not tempted to drop out of education.

It is also recognised that *information and communications technology* can help to achieve this goal by making learning more enjoyable and relevant to the hi-tech world that most Finns already inhabit. By the end of 1999 it was expected that more than 80 per cent of lower and upper comprehensives and more than 90 per cent of upper secondaries and vocational schools would be linked to the Internet. The government has established an Information Society Programme which it regards as a key policy priority. It wants 21st century Finns to have the basic knowledge and skills not only to understand ICT but use it as a tool in learning and research – at work and in their free time. Special efforts are being made to ensure that men and women have equal opportunities in this respect.

Inevitably, there is an element of pressure as well as support in the government's strategy to raise motivation levels and foster lifelong learning habits. Since 1996, young people under 25 with no vocational training have only been entitled to unemployment benefit if they have actively sought training but have been unable to find a suitable place. The fact that upper secondary and vocational schools are funded on a per-capita basis is a further inducement to keep students in the system as long as possible.

Schools are also being pressed to develop the learning skills – such as the ability to work autonomously – that young people will need in order to become lifelong learners. But it would be misleading to suggest that there is an even balance between pressure and support. The emphasis is clearly on the following positive inducements:

- *Financial support*: No fees are charged for upper secondary education and initial vocational education in Finland. Students are also entitled to free meals and healthcare and can apply for a package of financial assistance that is related to their needs. Municipalities also cover some students' travel expenses. The level of support that higher-education students receive is also dependent on their individual circumstances but it is not assumed that their parents will help to finance their studies.

- *Choice*: An unusual degree of freedom is now being offered to students at the end of the upper comprehensive stage. They can apply for a place in a school in another municipality – even at the other end of the country. As institutions have been legally obliged to co-operate with one another since January 1, 1999, students can choose to study simultaneously in both a vocational school and an upper secondary school that follows a general academic curriculum. They can also exert far more choice over what they study. Upper secondary students used to take 14 compulsory subjects and several optional subjects.

83

There was therefore only one lesson a week in most subjects. Now the school year is divided into five or six "periods" of the same length and the students determine which subjects they will study during each of them. Each subject is now allocated a minimum of five hours a week and is studied for only part of the year. About two-thirds of the curriculum remains compulsory, and choice is more limited in the smallest schools. Nevertheless, the introduction of a modular and non-graded (*i.e.* not tied to year groups) curriculum has opened up undreamed of possibilities. This is particularly true for upper secondary students in schools that have been involved in the Youth Education Experiment that is designed to draw the general and vocational sectors closer together. University-bound students in general schools have been able to interrupt their studies to pursue a hobby or interest in a vocational school. Vocational students have been spending part of the week studying a language, or other subjects, at a general school, and athletes have been able to take a break from their studies during term time to concentrate on sports training. Students are expected to complete 75 course modules – each of 38 hours – but they can stretch them over four years, or rush through them in two (very few choose this option) rather than complete their upper secondary schooling within the standard three-year period.

- *Advice and counselling:* The government acknowledges that young people may need more advice and counselling if they are to benefit fully from their new freedoms. However, every upper comprehensive, upper secondary and vocational school has a counsellor who can provide advice on studying, career paths and applying for the next stage of education. The fact that upper comprehensive school students can apply for places in up to five upper secondary institutions on a single form smoothes the transition from one stage to another. Finnish schools also have a large number of support personnel – such as social workers and nurses – who can help young people who are in danger of dropping out because of personal problems.

The Finns have a well-known saying, "All life is learning", and many adults evidently take it literally.

One student turned up for the first day of school wearing a T-shirt bearing the message: "I hate myself and I want to die."

Case study No. 1

Institution:	**Vipunen vocational school**
Location:	**Savonlinna, eastern Finland**

Teenagers who feel they are failures are being encouraged to adopt a more optimistic view of their future in a vocational school that offers an unusual degree of freedom, counselling and understanding.

Vipunen school is named after a mythical Finnish giant who knew the secrets of the boat-builder's art. It is an apt choice of name as Savonlinna, a summer tourist resort in eastern Finland, is at the centre of Europe's biggest lakeland region and boat-building is one of the courses that the school offers. Vipunen is part of the Savonlinna Vocational Institute, which is administered by nine local municipalities, but some students come from as far away as the north of Finland to follow its specialist courses.

Savonlinna has taken part in the Youth Education Experiment, which has allowed students in upper secondaries and vocational schools to mix and match courses. But it has been only a partial success so far in Savonlinna. About 40 of Vipunen's 500 students now opt for courses in an upper secondary school but there has been little movement in the opposite direction, partly because of time-tabling complications. Distance is a further obstacle. Two of the upper secondary school boys who have been working in Vipunen's wood-assembly department have to travel 45 km to the school.

Many Vipunen students, however, have little or no interest in academic study. Just under a fifth of them go straight onto a further course of study after leaving Vipunen (as military service is compulsory in Finland many students choose to do it immediately after completing the upper-secondary stage of their education), but the majority have more modest ambitions, particularly in their first year. The school's head says that many students arrive feeling that they are complete failures. A local newspaper photographed one of her students turning up for the first day of school wearing a T-shirt bearing the message: "I hate myself and I want to die." She has hung the photograph in her office and it is a constant reminder of the scale of the challenge that the school faces.

The first objective is often to build self-esteem – a responsibility that is shared by teachers, craft supervisors, the school's student counsellor and the social worker. The first year is regarded as the key year in this respect. If the staff's efforts are successful then concentration and motivation can be improved.

85

A range of motivational strategies has proved successful in the craft departments, which help the school to cover 20 per cent of its costs by providing services for local businesses. In the wood-assembly section, which earns the equivalent of US$175 700 a year from private contracts, the supervising craftsmen have stimulated students' interest by asking them to design and build furniture. The opportunity to use the most sophisticated computer-controlled wood-cutting machinery is a further incentive for working in the section, as is the paid holiday employment that is available in the summer.

Student hairdressers, who supplement their student grants by running a holiday salon at the college, and young boat-builders who take on private commissions in their spare time, are also partly motivated by the prospect of financial reward. But both sets of students appear proud of their newly-acquired skills. The hairdressers' interest in their work has also been enhanced by international exchanges with schools in Northern Ireland, Belgium and Sweden. In the vehicle repair section the students seem to be motivated by the opportunity to work alongside older mechanics, both in the college and on extended workplacements, and progress is acknowledged by the award of more responsibilities. As their skills grow the students are allowed to work on newer and more expensive vehicles. Similarly, in the metalwork section, students have been stimulated by the invitation to work on one of the biggest and most technically-demanding contracts the school has won – the construction of a vehicle that is used to lay paths in mines.

The school's head speaks metaphorically about the search for the most effective motivators. "The door is in a different place in the wall for every student. When we find it we look for the key rather than try to kick it open." The Vipunen staff also believe in allowing students to follow their own interests and try to be as flexible as possible. Some students have consequently been allowed to start and finish their school day later than their peers.

Vipunen students have been taking part in a pilot study – "A Bridge from Vocational Education to Working Life" funded by the European Social Fund – which has enabled them to spend between 10 and 12 weeks on work placements. Longer placements have been arranged for mechanics who prefer to train in a commercial garage. The relatively low drop-out rate indicates that the school's flexible approach works (although the local unemployment rate of 21 per cent is another incentive to remain in school). The fact that two of the local employers questioned during the visit had recruited several Vipunen students and were happy with their attitude towards work is another positive sign. But a third employer said that some students had failed to turn up for work placements. This is hardly surprising as the school caters for some very difficult students. But it does suggest that Vipunen, despite an unusual degree of staff commitment, has so far found only some of the answers it has been seeking.

Case study No. 2

Institution: **Kuninkaanhaka upper comprehensive school**

Location: **Pori, western Finland**

Fifteen-year-olds who drop out of main stream education and then fall through one safety net find that a second one – in the form of an unusual workshop school – is waiting to catch them.

Pori is a large industrial town on the west coast of Finland. Its two harbours and airport offer good connections to other Baltic states but it has been plagued by unemployment for years. In some areas of Pori up to 40 per cent of adults are out of work. Kuninkaanhaka, a 400-pupil school that specialises in sport, has to cope with the social consequences. Over the past five years it has introduced a range of programmes that promote healthy lifestyles, non-violent behaviour and lifelong learning. Some have been supported by the Pori school board, others by the Board of Education in Helsinki and the National Research and Development Centre for Welfare and Health.

Pori's youth crime statistics are not unusually high but there is concern about the polarising social structure, alcoholism and drug abuse. Motivating the children of disintegrating families is another formidable task for the staff who regard Kuninkaanhaka as a fairly typical Pori school. Class sizes range from 22 to 27 and all but five of the 40 teachers are women. Like the other Finnish case-study schools, Kuninkaanhaka also has a team of specialist support staff: a counsellor, social worker and nurse. But the headteacher says that the canteen staff and other non-teaching staff also try to act as caring role models.

One particularly important role model is the trainee teacher and musician who tutors six boys with a challenging mix of learning and behaviour problems. His "classroom" is in a highly unusual setting – a bomb shelter under the nearby municipal swimming pool. The boys spend 16 hours a week (spread over four days) with him and a further 14 hours in the main school. He invariably sets them only one subject a week and allows them to spend about an hour a day recording music, using a computer or playing football.

The school is sensitive about the location of these classes, aware that it could be seen as a semi-custodial environment. The head teacher explains that the bomb-shelter was chosen simply because there was no accommodation in the school. In any case, as the boys spend almost half their week in mainstream classes they are able to maintain friendships and follow the general curriculum. As the experiment has only been running since November 1998 it is impossible to say whether this approach works but there appeared to be a general improvement in the boys' grades as a result of the more individual coaching they received during the first six months of the initiative. The younger students were consequently expected to return to the main school full-time after the 1999 summer break.

If they had not been considered capable of rejoining their classmates the boys might have been referred to the workshop school a few hundred yards from Kuninkaanhaka school. It takes up to 10 students – usually aged 15 and 16 – who have exhausted their other education options. The school is based in a small house next to a workshop for unemployed young adults and is run by a former probation officer who offers his students an unorthodox curriculum that draws heavily on the teachings of Paolo Freire. The workshop school year is divided into four interlocking sections. In the first, the head concentrates on their individual needs because many students turn up at his school convinced that they cannot learn. He then switches to language and media studies. In the third "term" he focuses on the environment, particularly of Pori, and then finally he deals with cultures, what the Finns might learn from other cultures and give to them in return. He teaches the students through practical activities in the workshops or holds informal tutorials in his "classroom", which looks more like a youth club, with settees instead of wooden chairs, and no desks. He also takes his students into a remote area of forest once a year and shows them how to make traditional weapons. "The last time we planned to take live chickens for food but eventually had to compromise and take frozen ones instead", he said.

In five years, 45 troubled teenagers have passed through the workshop school and only one, a young man, proved to be beyond its help (he later committed suicide – Finland's male suicide rate is far and away the highest in Europe). The rest are continuing their education or have managed to find jobs even though youth unemployment has been relatively high in Finland in recent years. It is an achievement that the head takes understandable pride in.

Case study No. 3

Institution:	Mankkaa upper comprehensive school
Location:	Espoo, southern Finland
Starting date:	1991

New technology may not always be as liberating as its advocates contend but a school in Finland's second biggest city is demonstrating how it can free children and teachers from routine classroom life.

Mankkaa school is a reminder of how wealthy Finland was at the end of the 1980s. This well-designed two-storey school is set in a birch wood and serves a socially-advantaged area of Espoo. Its teacher-student ratio is relatively generous: 30 staff (three of them part-timers) in a school of 350 13 to 15-year-olds. The school also has an above-average number of computers – 60 – and many were bought relatively recently.

Mankkaa was well-equipped when it opened in 1991 but it has been able to buy more computers by dispensing with one of the janitor posts (the work is now undertaken by students) and transferring the saving to the IT account. Students also take turns serving food in the canteen and do some cleaning. The primary aim is not to save money but to engender a sense of "responsibility" – the word that is said to sum up the school's philosophy. Students are encouraged to become autonomous learners and between 10 and 15 per cent of the timetable is given over to individual project work. The day is divided into double lessons of 90 minutes but in many classes the teacher addresses the students for perhaps 20 minutes. During the remainder of the lesson, students work on their own or in groups, and they particularly enjoy searching for information on the Internet.

Mankkaa school has found that the Internet is motivating girls who were once disinterested in computers. But some restraint has to be applied by the staff. A teacher of English and Swedish explained: "We try to let the students follow their interests, up to a point. If a project is on England and a student wants to focus on English horses that is all right. But if next month she is doing a project on Norway and suggests that she writes about Norwegian horses we steer her in another direction."

Because most students are used to working on their own it is relatively easy for teachers to offer individual attention to a child who is less motivated. A student counsellor is also available to provide advice and support, as is the school's social worker who also visits Mankkaa's feeder schools. Motivation problems can also be addressed by the team of subject teachers responsible for each of the three year groups. But lack of motivation does not appear to be a serious problem at Mankkaa, except in the Swedish language classes.

Virtually every child goes on to upper secondary education (under 30 per cent to vocational schools) but it is difficult to determine exactly how much of this success can be attributed to the school. The students undoubtedly enjoy the project work, and the responsibility they are given. However, some of Mankkaa's former students report that they are more stimulated by upper secondary school where they are given more say over what they study and are set more exacting work.

Innovation and effectiveness

The substantial body of research into motivation strategies that has been carried out in the United States (Kohn, 1994) suggests that the Finnish government and schools are laying sound foundations for lifelong learning by offering students:

- More choice.
- A more engaging and relevant curriculum.
- A safe educational community in which to discover and create.
- The support of adults who care about them as individuals.

However, it is difficult to reach firm conclusions about the effectiveness of the initiatives discussed earlier in this chapter for three reasons.

First, although the Finnish government generates a welter of education statistics there is relatively little data on the effectiveness – or failure – of its strategies for motivating teenagers. A new evaluation system, based on 5-10 per cent samples of the student population, should prove useful in this respect as it will measure not only academic achievement but the competencies and characteristics that are essential for lifelong learning. Unfortunately, it is still in the process of being introduced.

Secondly, several of the national initiatives and the school projects described are too recent to have been properly evaluated. Thirdly, many schools, such as Vipunen and Kuninkaanhaka, are involved in a range of projects aimed at increasing motivation and inculcating lifelong-learning habits. Vipunen is taking part in or has recently completed, eight national projects promoting either on-the-job learning or improved social relationships. It is also associated with six regional projects and seven international projects funded by the European Union. It is therefore virtually impossible to gauge the impact that any one of these has had.

Transferability of strategies

At a national level, perhaps the boldest development is the establishment of *non-graded upper-secondary schools* where students are not tied to particular year groups. As there have been experiments with non-graded schools in Finland since the 1980s they can no longer be described as innovative but they do appear to be motivating students. One 1995 study (Valijarvi and Tuomi, 1993) found that "school climate" is assessed more highly by students following a non-graded course. Such students also have better attitudes towards learning and more positive relationships with teachers. A second study (Van den Akker, 1996) reported that the new rhythm to the academic year helped to motivate students who preferred to concentrate on only a few subjects at a time.

Another reported advantage of the non-graded schools is that less able students do not have to repeat years (students simply drop a subject if they fail two successive modules). Regular changing of subjects and teachers also brings welcome variety to schoolwork, and motivation consequently increases at the start of each of the five or six "periods" in the academic year. It also appears that the non-graded curriculum provides the necessary base for lifelong learning as it obliges students to take responsibility for their own education and allows them to study at their own pace. Researchers have, however, found that motivation tends to wane towards the end of a study period, particularly if a student has chosen too many similar subjects. Moreover, not all students are motivated by the prospect of increased choice: some are happier with a ready-made curriculum.

The Youth Education Experiment, which has extended the choice of over-16s even further by allowing *simultaneous study in upper-secondary and vocational schools*, also appears to have stimulated some students. In a pilot project about 25 per cent of students took advantage of this opportunity, but it seems unlikely that this pattern will ever be followed by the majority of teenagers in sparsely-populated countries such as Finland where partner institutions can be many miles apart.

As explained earlier, the drive to expand *on-the-job learning* may also be balked by logistical problems. This initiative cannot be classified as innovative as many other countries are testing out similar strategies, but the length of the Finnish work placements (20 weeks in every three-year course) is ambitious. The fact that this work experience can be gained in other parts of Finland, or even in other countries, is bound to act as a further stimulus for some students. The increased prospect of being able to take a higher-education course after completing vocational school (the government has told the polytechnics that they should recruit 35 per cent of their students from the vocational sector) will also act as a spur.

The growing emphasis on *advice and counselling* on both academic and personal issues also seems likely to increase motivation. In upper comprehensive schools, a counsellor will talk to students for two hours a fortnight about such issues as learning how to learn. But again, there appear to be no statistics or research confirming that such interventions work (indeed the data on Finnish suicides suggest that even more personal counselling is needed). The same can be said about the individual school initiatives described in this chapter.

Nevertheless, it appears that Vipunen staff go to extreme lengths to tailor courses to suit students' individual interests. By no means all the Vipunen students appeared to be motivated, but without the support of the school's staff they would almost certainly be less ready for working life and adult society. It was, however, surprising to learn that students appear to be planning only one or two months' ahead. Although short-term goals are undoubtedly motivating for teenagers a longer perspective might also pay dividends.

91

Mankkaa School appears to be an almost ideal learning environment but it i one that only the best-resourced institutions could replicate exactly. Certair aspects of the Mankkaa philosophy could, however, be usefully transferred te schools in other countries – such as the emphasis on responsibility. Mankkaa's stu dents seemed unusually mature and self-sufficient and their general enthusiasm for individual computer-based project work does suggest that many of them may become lifelong learners. But research indicates that the project approach may be best-suited to schools in socially-advantaged districts. One 1995 Finnish study (Ahonen, 1996) concluded that independent study of this kind attracted just ove half of the students from more academic families but only 35 per cent of childrer whose parents had received only a basic education.

The project approach might therefore be less effective in some parts of Pori Kuninkaanhaka school has different needs and has had to seek quite radical solu tions. The bomb-shelter initiative may be short-lived but the idea of establishing semi-detached units for students who are in danger of dropping out is a sensible strategy that is being pursued in other countries. Expecting such students to become lifelong learners in any formal sense may be unrealistic, however. The head of the Kuninkaanhaka workshop school has a more modest goal: "To help them to be at peace with themselves and society."

Commentary

Anyone who is able to question the administrators, teachers and support staff involved in the initiatives described in this chapter cannot fail to be impressed by their determination to do the best for the current generation of Finnish teenagers. The evidence that the motivational strategies are working is mainly anecdotal but it would be unwise to disregard the Finnish approaches because of the lack of data.

The needs of the brightest comprehensive school pupils may not always be fully catered for but it does appear that great efforts are being made to motivate the least-advantaged children and ensure that they have a stake in the hi-tech society of the future. Finnish educational policy-makers have for years been work-ing towards "equity with variety" but now that they have begun to break down the barriers between academic and vocational upper secondary schools they are much closer to achieving that goal than many other countries.

Bibliography

AHONEN, S. (1996),
   History Knowledge as a Learning Result.

JAKKU-SIHVONEN, R. and LINDSTROM, A. (1996),
   Is Equality a Reality in Finnish Comprehensive Schools, National Board of Education, Helsinki.

KANNAS, L. (1995),
   Health, Wellbeing and Enjoyment of Schoolchildren, National Board of Education, Helsinki.

KOHN, A. (1994),
   "The risk of rewards", ERIC *Digest*.

KORPINEN, E. (1990),
   The Self-image in Comprehensive School, Institute for Education and Research Publication.

LINNAKYLA, P. et al. (1996),
   How do pupils Experience School? The Quality of School Life and its Improvement in the '90s.

MINISTRY OF LABOUR (1998),
   Employment Action Plan.

OECD (1998),
   OECD Economic Surveys: Finland, Paris.

TUOMI, P. (1995),
   The Comprehensive School Pupil's Self-image as Learner.

VALIJARVI, J. and TUOMI, P. (1993),
   Learning Environment and the students' Choices in the Senior Secondary School, University of Jyvaskyla.

VAN DEN AKKER, J. et al. (1996),
   The Modular Curriculum: A Senior Secondary School Study in Finland.

ICELAND

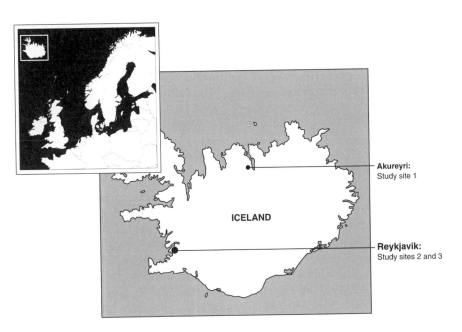

Akureyri:
Study site 1

ICELAND

Reykjavik:
Study sites 2 and 3

Land area in square kilometers: 103 000.

Total population (1998): 273 800.

Youth population – under 15 years (1998):
- 64 343,
- percentage of total population: 23.5%.

Youth unemployment (1998):
- 16-24 year-olds: 6.0%.

Percentage of 18-year-olds in education (1998): 67%.

Per capita GDP (1997 prices): 24 836 USD.

Birth rate per 1 000 population (1996): 16.1.

Sources: Labour Force Statistics: 1979-1998, OECD, Paris; *Annual National Accounts, Main Aggregates, Volume 1, 1999,* OECD, Paris; *Education at a Glance,* OECD Database 1999, Paris.

Country context

Education: Free compulsory schooling begins at the age of 6 in Iceland and ends at 16. Parents pay a fee for pre-school attendance while upper secondary students pay a small enrolment fee and buy their own textbooks. Responsibility for administering compulsory schools was switched in 1996 from the state to the municipalities. There are four types of upper secondary schools: academic, comprehensive, industrial-vocational and specialist schools. Upper secondary schools generally provide a four-year course and most use a system of unit credits. Vocational students have the right to take additional courses in preparation for higher education. New curriculum guidelines were introduced in the autumn of 1999 for both compulsory and upper-secondary systems. This reform is designed to prepare the Icelandic people for the knowledge economy. New curriculum areas emphasise life skills, science (following poor scores in the Third International Maths and Science Study – TIMSS) and information technology. English is being given preference to Danish as a first foreign language, and technology will be used to trigger innovations in vocational training.

Economy: After a long history of political ties with Denmark, Iceland became an independent republic in 1944. It has a homogeneous population of some 275 000, of which only 2-3 per cent are recent immigrants. Over half the population lives in the capital, Reykjavik, and the surrounding area. The country is divided into 123 municipalities, that have between 50 to more than 100 000 residents. In the 1970s and 80s there was high inflation associated with a steady increase in GNP but the inflation rate is now about 2 per cent. The fishing industry accounts for one-seventh of GNP, employs about one-eighth of the workforce and generates about 70 per cent of exports. The unemployment rate is very low at just over 2 per cent (1999) and in recent years there has been a marked fall in the number of young people who are out of work. Part-time employment is relatively easy to find and the economy has been growing quickly (OECD, 1998).

Student motivation issues

The main concern about student motivation in Iceland is the high level of drop-out from upper secondary school, which has been estimated at 30 per cent. A further 10 per cent of upper secondary students have still not graduated by the age of 22 (Jónasson, 1992). However, these figures are said to have fallen over the past 10 years following increased curriculum choice in upper secondary schools.

These figures, which are high in comparison with Iceland's Scandinavian neighbours also need to be considered in context. First, the rate of unemployment is low, and this, allied to a tradition in Iceland that students help to meet the costs of their own upper secondary schooling through part-time work, means that the value of spending further time at school needs to be very clear to them. Second, and importantly, as access to upper secondary education is very open, students can return easily after taking a break from schooling.

The limited research evidence shows that most students prefer academic courses to vocational training, since they believe that matriculation gives them an insurance for adult life (Bílddal, 1993). This view persists even though transferability from vocational to academic courses is assured and does not prejudice university entrance.

A 1992 study of 4 100 young adults born in 1969 (Jónasson and Jónsdottír, 1992) showed that 13 per cent of them had not completed any course of study since leaving lower secondary school. Asked why they did not continue with school, 50 per cent of this group reported lack of interest or boredom and 18 per cent mentioned lack of money. Forty per cent of the group had children, which proved to be a major reason for young women dropping out. However, over three-quarters of those who had children and those who did not were interested in further study, particularly if they could take practical subjects. The lack of choice in upper secondary schools, at the time the research was conducted, may help to explain these findings.

Research (Jónasson, 1992) has also revealed that students in less densely populated areas are less likely to attend upper secondary school. This is despite the fact that rural teenagers who do not complete upper secondary scored better marks than equivalent urban students at the end of their compulsory education. The need to move away from their community and the resulting financial costs are presumably implicated.

Further analysis of the 1969 cohort (Óskarsdottír, 1995) found that 25 per cent of young people who had dropped out of upper secondary schools had completed courses outside the state system, and many could see themselves taking vocational training courses in upper secondary schools. Furthermore, only 13 per cent of those who had dropped out claimed to dislike school (although other studies suggest this proportion is even lower – see Jónasson and Jónsdottír). School was more popular with girls than boys, but in this group both sexes preferred practical courses.

Other findings (Óskarsdottír, 1995) have revealed that drop-out is related to the final marks obtained at comprehensive school; the lower the marks the more likely the student is to drop out. The performance of students with low marks wa also correlated with the father's education level. Of those drop-outs who were working, the majority intended to continue their studies but many said that lack o money was an obstacle.

Truancy is also a significant problem in upper secondary school. Unsurprisingly, it has a negative effect on examination marks and is positively correlated with drop-out (Karlsson *et al.*, 1993). Bored students were also the ones most likely to truant. Violence and disruptive behaviour have also been linked with a lack o parental support and, of course, poor marks.

Research in Iceland (Sigurdardóttir, 1991) has also indicated that female students who take on part-time jobs to pay for their upper secondary school have more health problems than those who do not. Young women with jobs were found to smoke more, had more physical complaints and their attendance record wa poorer. They were more depressed, nervous and apprehensive and had lower self-esteem than non-working females. They also encountered more problems than male students who had part-time jobs.

In summary, drop-out is viewed as an important problem in Iceland. Some critics of the state education system see it as a sign that schools offer too little curriculum choice. It is also regarded as the key indicator of poor motivation among upper secondary students. However, it seems that many of the 30 per cent who drop out do so for reasons other than lack of motivation. On the whole, they report liking school, they want to study more, and some re-enter the education system one way or another, perhaps through the private business school. Lack of choice and a cultural preference for academic studies for which many are ill-suited are inhibiting factors. Interviews with students that were conducted during the course of the OECD visit suggest that lack of success, personal attention and low self-esteem, associated with unrealistic levels of aspiration, are further contributory factors. As we shall see policy approaches have been adopted to respond to these issues.

Main policy approaches

The government of Iceland is concerned about the drop-out statistics. Certainly, if 30 per cent of the student population fail to complete upper secondary education this does not bode well for the country's future. However, a number o government education policies could raise motivation levels. Within the comprehensive review of education the government is targeting six main areas: governance, schools, curriculum, pedagogy, personal development and teacher training.

Governance – Transferring the administration of compulsory education from the state to the municipalities should allow the system to be more responsive to local conditions. The ministry has retained control of upper secondary schools but is allowing them to compete for students. It has also indicated that upper secondary schools may lose per-capita funds if students drop out. This incentive, it is hoped, will encourage schools to pay more attention to the needs of less motivated students. The new preparatory courses for higher education introduced in 1999 may motivate students to stay on in education or return to school. In future, there will also be more freedom for private education to open up both at upper secondary and higher education levels with appropriate quality controls.

Schools – At present, some compulsory schools still work in shifts in the morning and afternoon. A building programme will make this unnecessary by 2004 and should substantially improve the conditions of work. The number of periods taught will also be increased. This should raise standards and give students the skills they need to cope with upper secondary school. Since the 1970s, evening schools attached to some upper secondary schools have been offering courses for adults. Students over 18 may now attend these courses, and this has proven to be a very popular option. But the ease of access to upper secondary education throughout life has also been criticised for discouraging teenagers from staying on to complete their studies. A 1996 law addressed this issue but further ways of tackling this problem without losing the enviable flexibility of the present system are being considered. Funds for developmental schemes are available to encourage schools to experiment with different means of motivating students. Some of these schemes have proved very successful and have been extended to other schools. Two of them are described later in this chapter. Distance education is also being expanded since this shows great promise for increasing the motivation of those who are geographically isolated. There has, however, been a long-standing equity policy to offer foundation programmes all over the country and relocation grants are available for students. In lower secondary schools, students are often taught in mixed-ability groups although there is some setting. This allows students to follow the curriculum at different speeds. A few lower secondary schools allow especially diligent students to take course units at a nearby upper secondary school. Four branches of study may be followed at upper secondary school: vocational, academic, general and fine arts, which should all be adapted to meet individual student needs. Each branch must provide access to further or higher education – either directly or through additional studies.

Curriculum – This is undergoing substantial reform by the ministry to make it more relevant and broad. Through greater flexibility, choice, individualisation and special help, poorly motivated and weaker students will be given the opportunity to gain the skills necessary for higher levels of education. More options will be available but courses will be rationalised. The new curriculum guidelines, implemented in the autumn of 1999, included a section on life-skills, which will be a compulsory course in upper secondary schools. Closer links between academic and vocational training are also planned so that students may develop skills in both areas. Ties between vocational training courses and business will be strengthened with the increase in occupational courses offered and participation of business in shaping educational demand. There is also discussion about introducing diplomas fo one-year courses rather than just on the completion of upper secondary school.

Pedagogy – It is recognised that the current style of teaching at the upper secondary level can demotivate students. Experimental schemes have therefore been introduced, and two are described later in this chapter. Both get to grips in different ways with the problems presented by the rather fragmented, subject-based teaching that is offered in many upper secondary schools. Methods emphasising project work, teaching through more concrete approaches, greater individualisation and student self-evaluation, are being developed. An effort is also being made to change student-grouping practices in order to enhance self-esteem. Information technology-based distance-learning approaches are being introduced and are proving very successful.

Personal development – The Icelandic government has recognised that educational success is not only determined by schools but is also related to a student's personal life and family background. As in other countries, the high divorce rates in Iceland and low family incomes can be very disturbing for some students and may interfere with their motivation to work well at school. Efforts are therefore being made to upgrade and co-ordinate the support that families and schools receive from social services and improve the quality and quantity of counselling available for students. Academic and career counselling are to be substantially increased and social worker involvement is being expanded in some municipalities to help students with their personal problems. Contact between schools and parents is also seen as a way to prevent drop-out.

Teacher training and in-service education of teachers (INSET) – These are regarded as key elements of the education reforms. Although teacher-training colleges retain their independence in terms of course content, the ministry has involved them in the planning of the new curriculum guidelines in the hope that a partnership approach will influence the training they offer.

Support for INSET that is related to the new curriculum guidelines is also being planned.

"The main concern about student motivation is the 30 per cent drop-out rate from upper secondary school."

The distance learning students appreciate the freedom to work when they choose to, and the "next day" feedback they receive.

STUDY SITES

Case study No. 1

Institution:	**The College of Vocational Training in Akureyri – distance education programme**
Location:	**Akureyri, North Iceland**
Starting date:	**1994**

Many people who are motivated to study find that practical obstacles, such as family commitments or physical handicap, stand in the way. This successful distance education programme is clearing those barriers away.

Akureyri upper secondary school is 80 kilometres from the Arctic Circle and about 45 minutes by plane from Reykjavik. Vocational education in this part of Iceland has been developing for about a century and has been slowly brought together in this school. Established in 1984, it now provides a full range of subjects for more than 1 000 students.

Over the past six years the school has established a successful distance-education service that aims to provide the same curriculum coverage and identical exam options and requirements as the school's regular programme. The distance-education students can therefore continue their education into the university sector.

Students working *via* distance education fall into three groups. First, there are those who for geographical reasons cannot attend an upper secondary school, such as those living in remote villages, or abroad. Second, are those who for social or personal reasons cannot attend a school: parents with heavy family responsibilities, students with disabilities, shift workers or people with unusual life styles. One student is a national judo champion training for the Olympics. The third group includes those attending a school with a limited range of courses. Another student was studying Spanish with the help of a teacher living in Reykjavik. The students are responsible for a proportion of their teaching fees, which are not cheap, but because there are no accommodation, travel and subsistence expenses the overall cost to students is lower.

The distance-education programme has been developed in meticulous detail by its organisers who have assembled a talented and committed teaching team. It has a far better student: teacher ratio than the regular programme (9:1 rather than 18:1) and the materials used can operate within the limits of the average home computer. Clearly this is a system that works well technically; an essential pre-requisite of any distance-education programme. But the positive impact on student motivation is also unequivocally clear. The programme's drop-out rate is about half that of the school as a whole. However, it must be borne in mind that the programme enrols older students on average and the course organisers noted that younger students are not as motivated and are more likely to drop out. Other factors may also be implicated, such as the special nature of the distance-education population sampled and the fact that this is an experimental programme.

Nevertheless, the students appreciate the freedom to work when they choose to, and the "next day" feedback they receive. Assignments are often marked by the computer and students may keep going until they get the correct answers. Everyone therefore enjoys some success. Furthermore, this method inhibits the student from cheating and not attending classes. All this helps students to find learning "fun". It also increases self-discipline and independence and makes them feel that teachers care about them as individuals. Surveys have shown that 60 per cent of students report isolation as a disadvantage. The three students who were interviewed agreed with this but pointed out that a student may also be isolated in a regular upper secondary school.

Case study No. 2

Institution:	Borgarholt Upper Secondary School
Location:	Reykjavík
Starting date:	1996

Potential drop-outs are learning how to improve their work habits and skills on an experimental course that offers new teaching methods, a tailor-made curriculum and the chance to build their self-esteem.

At Borgarholt School, a special course of study is being developed to combat dropping out. It is intended for students who have not decided what to study, or who need to improve their knowledge of core subjects in order to join the academic stream. It is viewed as an experimental approach that could become a model for developing general studies within new curriculum guidelines. Applicants for the course are often rejects from other schools.

The course is in many ways like other general courses on offer in Iceland's upper secondary schools. The required course covers Icelandic, English, mathematics, sports and special subjects which give students a fuller understanding of themselves, society, business methods, the environment, Iceland's place on the world stage, and civic and family responsibilities. They also choose from a number of academic or practical options.

Borgarholt school, however, has been experimenting with different teaching methods and staff organisation to offer students individual curriculum "menus". The overall goal is to tackle poor motivation by increasing students' self-esteem, ndependence and interest in lifelong learning. The school tries to do this through nvolving them more fully in decision-making about their courses of study and offering them teaching grounded in practical experiences. The aim is to show students that they can learn effectively and succeed. It is recognised that many of these students have personal problems that can hinder their educational progress. Counselling is provided at the school and is supported by specialists at the University of Iceland. Teachers are also encouraged to be more sensitive and flexible in their dealings with students.

In fact, flexibility is a strong feature of this approach. The class schedule can be interrupted so that students can concentrate on one subject for an entire day or even for a week. Teachers may work together in teams and project work is commonplace. Workshops and field trips are also used to enliven the coursework.

Mathematics teachers try to respond to students' different knowledge levels. After a relatively traditional introduction, students are encouraged to apply the maths they have learned in practical exercises such as map reading and the use of navigational aids.

In English lessons, the same skills are taught as to all other students, but there is more emphasis on creative work and assignments are more demanding. Informal comparisons with students in standard settings suggest that those in the experimental groups structure their essays better and earn higher grades.

The course focusing on personal and societal issues covers the Environment and Pollution, Take a Global View, and Look at the Media. Students also learn about "deep feelings" and the implications for their future life. A typical week's work includes an introduction to a topic by a teacher, followed by a brainstorming session. Groups then organise and focus their research questions and gather data from a wide variety of sources such as the library, Internet and interviews. Data will then be analysed and written up and the results presented to and evaluated by the whole group, a process that emphasises communication skills.

This approach has multiple benefits for unmotivated students. It gives them a different learning environment that offers group work, personal responsibility, organisational and presentational skills, freedom to make mistakes and to learn from them, and self-knowledge through personal evaluation. They learn how to improve their work habits and skills. They also learn that effort pays dividends and allows them to shine.

There are lessons here for both teachers and schools. This kind of approach can lead to noisy classrooms with much activity but teachers have to learn to let go and allow students to make mistakes. They must also improve their classroom-management skills, since students often need quietening down after such sessions. Furthermore, they must learn to work collaboratively with colleagues and meet regularly to develop course goals, plan lessons, develop materials and discuss individual students.

The individualised approaches that the teachers use are creating stronger ties with students than is normal in Icelandic upper secondary schools. Greater trust develops and this is enhanced by regular counselling, individual tutorials each semester, and weekly written communication between students and teacher. The students are encouraged to send their teacher a note about any problems they may be experiencing and the teacher writes a response on the back. Privacy is an important aspect of these exchanges.

So, are the increased pressures on the school and individual teachers worth it? The relatively low drop-out rate of 16 per cent in 1998-99 suggests that they are. The teachers themselves were convinced that the course helped to prevent drop-out although they admitted that motivation was still low and standards were not high enough.

In general, the students who were interviewed confirmed these evaluations (30 students from the previous and current year were questioned in groups of 10) inevitably, there were some dissenting voices but students liked the team-teaching approach, and they felt that the personal contact was good and led to trust. They also said that being in a group of fellow students whom they knew gave them confidence to speak and that project work developed *esprit de corps*.

Case study No. 3

Institution:	VT business and computer school
Location:	Reykjavík
Starting date:	1996

Rebuilding the self-confidence and skills of women students who may have been out of the job market for years is not an easy task. But this private school believes it has a general office studies course that does just that.

The VT business and computer school was founded in 1974 to train secretaries. Today it is a private school owned by the "Electricians' Re-education Committee". The school offers four job-related programmes lasting 30 weeks, on general office studies, finance and accounting studies, marketing and sales studies and computer studies. Next year, five new programmes will be added. The school is located in a modern building on a commercial estate in Reykjavik and is extremely well-equipped with computers and other modern teaching equipment.

The school's main goal is to enable students to follow specialist courses that will increase their job prospects. This is partly achieved through the 10-day job-training placements that have been established through the school's business links. They allow students to apply the skills they have learned in school in a real working environment and this hands-on experience increases the possibility of finding a job in the future.

Since 1994, the student body has grown from 75 to 282. Ninety-five per cent are women: either young students or more mature females who are returning to study after a period of family life. To qualify for the general office studies programme, the student must be at least 18 years of age and have completed lower secondary education (up to the 10th grade). For the other programmes a diploma from an upper secondary school is required and sometimes additional job experience. Potential students must therefore have exhibited some staying power. Some of the general office course students we met had dropped out of upper secondary school but it was often because of other attractive alternatives such as travel or the opportunity to study abroad.

Although the school is private, it is claimed that the costs are average for education of this sort. Fees are paid by the students and bank loans are available at special rates negotiated by the school. Students attend one of three three-hour sessions run in the morning, afternoon and evening and are expected to do two to three hours' homework each day. Students must have an 80 per cent attendance to register for the examination, which is a traditional model with 70 per cent of the overall mark based on written papers and 30 per cent on continuous assessment and homework assignments. All aspects of the service offered by the school are evaluated by the students at the end of the course, and the information is fed back to the management. The school accentuates the importance of being a real working environment and its teaching methods encourage self-reliance.

The teachers themselves are far from ordinary. The three we met had backgrounds in golf coaching, special education and theology. In addition, the school does not require its teachers to be formally trained and the system of employment allows for many short-term contracts and invited speakers. The teachers pointed out that many of the students, while being motivated, have low self-esteem. This was confirmed by several past and present students of varying ages. They argued that adults want short, intensive courses of the kind offered by the VT school even though they are not necessarily hoping to find work. The students also appreciated the intimacy of the school. They claimed that upper secondary schools did not provide the necessary experience in computing and although they enjoyed upper secondary school they did not like the courses it provided. These students were enjoying their work, felt that their prospects had improved, and had recovered their self-confidence following a long period without work.

The general office studies course offers training in Icelandic, English, bookkeeping, customs and excise reports, computer use, and management and organisation. But it is also designed to increase students' initiative, creative powers and social skills. The school uses the Dale Carnegie method for encouraging self-expression in larger groups (see Carnegie, 1956). Students are said to develop great self-esteem through success on the course – even those who have dropped out of the upper secondary system or are failures from the regular system. The drop-out rate from the school is very low and 60 per cent of its former students find jobs immediately after leaving the course. However, many students do not wish to find work and often begin families or continue their education.

Completion of the general office studies programme does not provide direct access to further education as it is classed as a short, vocational upper secondary course that does not count as a partial qualification for university entry. Nevertheless, the school clearly enjoys a good reputation and 30 per cent of the students attending do so because of personal recommendation. An employment agency also recommends it. The VT business school is a dynamic environment that offers great possibilities for those who want to work hard. Its dynamism is reflected in not only its teaching methods but the ever-changing nature of the courses on offer. For instance, the "over 67" course caters for senior citizens who want to use computers for tax returns, home banking, and even games.

* * *

Innovation and effectiveness

It is clear that the Ministry of Education, Science and Culture is making serious efforts to address the drop-out problem. The hope is that the experimental programmes it supports may be transferable to other schools throughout the country. At present there appear to be few formal evaluations of these efforts but the curriculum project at Borgarholt school has only a 16 per cent drop-out rate and the distance-education programme claims an even lower rate.

Discussions with students provide further anecdotal evidence of the effectiveness of these approaches, but some problems remain. At the Borgarholt school the students were aged 16-18 and certainly displayed elements of teenage *ennui*. Many were positive about the school but others were unimpressed by what the future had in store for them and revealed quite unrealistic aspirations. One, for instance, oscillated between a career as a hairdresser and a psychiatrist.

The distance-education students who were interviewed were older and certainly not diffident. None the less, they were all drop-outs from upper secondary school and it is unlikely that they would be continuing with education without this programme. Furthermore, they undoubtedly enjoyed this method of working.

Whether it would work more generally for unmotivated students, for example at the Borgarholt school, remains open to question, but the emphasis on choice, individualisation, success and quick feedback suggests that it might.

The students at the business school were also adults who were returning to study for particular purposes, and although some of them lacked self-esteem they did not appear to be especially unmotivated. The school provided efficiently for their needs, and work seemed to be available for those who wished it. Many went on to further study and this may indicate that lifelong learning objectives were being achieved.

Commentary

The government of Iceland has strong egalitarian and quality expectations for its students and systemic reforms are being initiated to tackle the key problem areas. Upper secondary education has many advantages. There is choice, students can leave and re-enter more or less at will throughout life, and there are no age constraints. A broad range of academic and vocational courses can be taught in the same institutions. However, the traditional method of organisation (the unit credit system) appears to fragment students and the methods of teaching are too theoretical. These arrangements only work well for students with a natural academic bent. The majority of vocational training tends to be too theoretical for the many students who would like to follow practical courses.

For many students, this results in a loss of self-confidence, a lack of trust and a feeling that they are not treated as individuals. Additionally, the rhythm and pace of schools often fail to take account of other pressures in their lives, such as working to keep themselves in school. The new reforms and the experimental programmes that are being developed by very enthusiastic and dedicated staff have the potential to remedy such problems and fulfil the government's mission of "Still better schools – Their right is our duty".

Bibliography

BÍLDDAL, S. (1993),
"Hugmyndir nemenda um nám og störf", Paper for education and culture, University o Iceland.

CARNEGIE, D. (1956),
How to Develop Self-confidence and Influence People by Public Speaking, Pocket Book, New York.

JÓNASSON J.T. (1992),
Námsferill og námslok í framhaldsskóla. N Menntamál, Vol. 10:3, pp. 22-23.

JÓNASSON, J.T. and JÓNSDÓTTIR, G.A. (1992),
Námsferill í framhaldsskóla – Helstu í durstödur, Report for the Ministry of Education, Science and Culture, Social Science Research Institute, University of Iceland.

KARLSSON, T., SIGURDARDÓTTIR, G. and THORLINDSSON, T. (1993),
Skróp nemenda í framhaldsskólum og tengsl vid adra thaetti í skóla, lífsstíl og andlega lídan, Uppeldi og menntum – Tímarit KHÍ, Vol. 2, pp. 62-85.

OECD (1998),
OECD Economic Surveys: Iceland, Paris.

ÓSKARSDÓTTIR, G.G. (1995),
The Forgotten Half: Comparison of Drop-outs and Graduates in their Early Work Experience – The Icelandic Case, Social Science Institute, University of Iceland, Reykjavík.

SIGURDARDÓTTIR, G. (1991),
Göfgar vinna med námi? Nidurstödur rannsóknar á tháttum tengdum vetrarvinnu framhaldsskólanema, Rannsóknarrit 1, Institute for Educational Research.

IRELAND

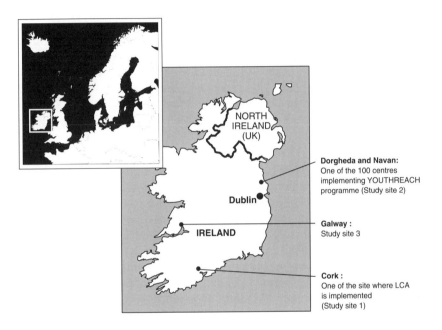

Dorgheda and Navan:
One of the 100 centres
implementing YOUTHREACH
programme (Study site 2)

Galway :
Study site 3

Cork :
One of the site where LCA
is implemented
(Study site 1)

Land area in square kilometers: 70 000.

Total population (1998): 3 705 000.

Youth population – under 15 years (1998):
- – 833 625,
- – percentage of total population: 22.5%.

Youth unemployment (1998):
- – 15-24 year-olds: 11.5%.

Percentage of 18-year-olds in education (1998): 71%.

Per capita GDP (1997 prices): 20 634 USD.

Birth rate per 1 000 population (1996): 13.4.

Sources: Labour Force Statistics: 1979-1998, OECD, Paris; Annual National Accounts, Main Aggregates, Volume 1, 1999, OECD, Paris; Education at a Glance, OECD Database 1999, Paris.

Country context

Education: Almost one million children and young people are enrolled in full-time education in Ireland. Currently, education is compulsory from the ages of 6 to 15, but there is a proposal in the Education (Welfare) Bill 1999 to raise the age to 16. In the 1997-98 school year, 52 per cent of four-year-olds and 100 per cent of five-year-olds were in the formal school system. About 80 per cent of young people complete second-level education. The educational attainments of those in the labour force are, however, distributed very unevenly on an age, social class and area basis (Department of Education and Science, 1998). There is growing provision for adult and continuing education, but free secondary education came to Ireland in 1967, later than to other OECD countries. The country therefore has well-educated young people and poorly-educated older people. This helps to explain why the OECD's International Adult Literacy Survey found that about 25 per cent of the Irish population scored at the lowest level of literacy. At best, this group performed tasks that required the reader to locate a simple piece of information in a text.

Economy: The effects of the economic boom in Ireland over the past few years have been ricocheting around almost every aspect of public life. Ireland may have caught up with the rest of Europe, but the suddenness of it all has caught politicians and planners by surprise and thrown up new challenges to the principle of partnership upon which social and economic developments have been based since the early 1980s. Growth rates jumped to 8 per cent from 1994 onwards and the unemployment rate has plummeted from 18 to below 7 per cent. Instead of multiple applicants for jobs, there are shortages of staff in areas such as catering, teleservices, computing, financial services and nursing. The shortages in some sectors are so serious that, in 1999, the state's training and employment agency, FÁS, embarked on a Jobs Ireland campaign abroad to build up a data base of 10 000 people who might like to work in the country. Irish and other EU citizens were targeted as part of the campaign. The boom has reversed the emigration pattern of decades. For the past few years Ireland has experienced net immigration of about 10 000 a year.

Student motivation issues

School attendance is a good barometer of student motivation. A recent study published by the Economic and Social Research Institute showed that the average-drop-out rate of 12 to 15-year-olds was 4.5 per cent, although rates in different schools varied from virtually zero to 41 per cent (Smyth, 1999). The rate is higher in schools where pupils come from predominantly working-class backgrounds and have parents with lower levels of education. It is also strongly related to the ability mix of the school, with higher drop-out where pupils are of lower ability. Highly streamed schools have greater drop-out rates among 16 to 18-year-olds. Early school-leaving is also associated with higher rates of absenteeism in the school as a whole. Unsurprisingly, those who tend to drop out include traveller (gypsy) families, the less academically inclined, and learners with disabilities. Data collected by the Department of Education and Science also show that boys are less likely than girls to complete secondary schooling (73: 83 per cent).

In 1995, it was estimated that over a quarter of young people in Ireland left school with either inadequate or no qualifications (National Economic and Social Forum, 1997). Of a cohort of approximately 65 000 who left school in that year:

- 2 200 gained no qualification (12 to 15-year-olds).
- 7 900 left with only the Junior Certificate (15-year-olds).
- 2 100 left with the Junior Certificate and a Vocational Preparation and Training qualification.
- 7 200 left at 17 or 18 with an inadequate Leaving Certificate (fewer than five D grades).

All secondary school students follow the same three-year junior cycle curriculum. The Junior Certificate was introduced in 1989 to provide a unified programme for those aged 12 to 15 and they sit a national public examination at the end of the three-year cycle. Most students complete a further two or three years in the senior cycle. There is an optional Transition year that is chosen by about half the students nationally. It has been described as an opportunity to get off the "academic treadmill" and schools use this bridging year in different ways. It can be a maturing year for weaker students, provide work experience and/or engagement in community projects, and offer short non-examination courses that might not otherwise get covered. Some schools insist that all their students do the Transition year, others offer it to a limited number of students. If they are not taking this bridging year, students can go directly into the two-year Leaving Certificate programme.

A predictable side-effect of the booming economy is that large numbers of secondary school students are working part-time, especially in the cities where shops, restaurants and bars offer plenty of opportunities. Legislation limiting the hours that young people can work is openly flouted by employers who are eager

111

to take on students, some of whom are tempted to leave education to work full-time. This is one of the factors making the government target of 90 per cent completing the upper secondary cycle difficult to achieve.

Main policy approaches

In the past few years, successive governments have given high priority to the twin problems of early school-leaving and young people who are educationally disadvantaged. Three key principles underpin the Department of Education and Science's commitment to the disadvantaged: continuity of concern; a holistic approach; and an area-based strategy. The underlying concepts are prevention, support, parental involvement, integration of services, and targeting of services. The assumption is that offering a rich variety of educational experiences will motivate students to remain in the system and achieve qualifications that will equip them for life and for lifelong learning. The range of initiatives includes the following:

- *Pre-School Early Start Programme*: This early-years initiative is aimed at selected disadvantaged areas and was established in 1994. The aims are to expose young children to a programme that will enhance their overall development, prevent school failure and offset the effects of educational disadvantage. The pre-school is an integral part of the primary school to which it is attached and operates within the general framework of the primary system. Each pre-school employs qualified primary teachers and qualified childcare assistants. Parental involvement is a fundamental part of the programme.

- *Home-School Community Liaison Programme*: The objective of this scheme is to engage the skills, experience and knowledge of parents and teachers to enhance the quality of children's education. The terms of the scheme, which was established in 1990, require schools in disadvantaged areas to deploy a teacher as co-ordinator with the full-time task of developing relationships between schools, homes and communities.

- *Designation of schools in disadvantaged areas*: Schools with concentrations of pupils with particular characteristics are identified as needing special help. For instance, secondary schools with large numbers of under-achieving pupils are designated and measures introduced to boost motivation and achievement. All designated schools receive enhanced capitation grants. Some receive additional staffing and become eligible for inclusion in other initiatives. Primary schools have a lower maximum class size than the norm.

- The *"Breaking the Cycle"* initiative: Introduced in 1996, this gives additional support to primary schools in selected urban and rural areas that have high concentrations of children who are at risk of under-achieving because of their socio-economic backgrounds. This multi-faceted approach to meeting the needs of educationally-disadvantaged children involves a reduction in class size, curriculum adaptation, the development of school plans and additional resources. The initiative covers 33 schools in large urban settings and 123 small rural schools grouped in 25 clusters.

- A *retention initiative at second level*: Launched in 1999, it aims to keep pupils in those schools that draw up a plan or agreement with the Department of Education and Science. A key requirement is that the school becomes a partner in a multi-agency approach; the school is not seen as the sole arbiter of strategy. The initiative is based on the principle of providing resources to schools to implement measures identified by them. This represents a departure from the traditional pattern of designing national initiatives and requiring schools to implement them. Forty schools are included in the initiative's first year of operation.

- *Education welfare*: The legislation that proposes raising the school-leaving age from 15 to 16 also calls for the establishment of an Educational Welfare Service to support and track families and children experiencing difficulties with school attendance. The legislation is also designed to improve attendance monitoring in schools, and ensure that poor attenders are offered appropriate placements, which could be in a YOUTHREACH centre (see project description later in this chapter). The legislation envisages that where 16 to 18-year-olds leave school to work, their employers will register them with the service so they can be supported and encouraged to continue their education or training. Part-time options are being developed in a number of programmes.

- *The Junior Certificate School Programme*: An alternative approach to the Junior Certificate that is designed to whet students' appetite for learning. It is aimed at the potential early school-leaver and is also used for other students who have difficulty in coping with the junior cycle curriculum. The teachers adapt the curriculum to make the whole school experience more meaningful for those students who are at risk. The emphasis is on the process of learning rather than on a terminal examination, on what students can do rather than on what they cannot do. One of the basic tenets of the programme is that every student is capable of making progress in learning and that this progress should be acknowledged. A profiling system is used to provide this affirmation of learning.

- *The Leaving Certificate Applied*: Introduced in 1995, it is a distinct form of the Leaving Certificate. Its fundamental goal is to prepare pupils for the transition from the world of school to adult and working life. This cross-curricular programme is offered in modules, with ongoing assessments. It includes vocational preparation, vocational education and general education. Students undertake a number of tasks, which are examined over two years. Credits are awarded for successful completion of the modules, for student tasks and for the final exams. The exam at the end of year two accounts for one third of the overall marks. About 3 per cent of senior-cycle students take the Applied programme (see following project description).

- YOUTHREACH: This initiative is targeted at 15 to 18-year-olds who have left school without qualifications or vocational training. It has two phases:

    - The foundation phase to help overcome learning difficulties, develop self-confidence and a range of competencies essential for further learning.

    - The progression phase, which provides for more specific development through a range of education, training and work-experience options.

  The programme is provided under local management in more than 100 out-of-school centres throughout the country. It places strong emphasis on literacy and numeracy, communications, information technology and personal development. It is certified by the National Council for Vocational Awards.

- *Vocational Training Opportunities Scheme* (VTOS): This scheme provides second-chance education and training for over 21-year-olds who have been in receipt of unemployment payments for at least six months, or are entitled to a lone parent's allowance, or a disability payment. Dependent partners of unemployed people are also eligible. The programme offers a variety of vocational options, focusing on new-technology skills, vocational skills, enterprise training, personal development and general studies. Courses cover basic education, the Leaving Certificate and further education. The government allocated more than IEP 26 million (US$34 715 687) to this scheme in 1998. Participants receive a training allowance in lieu of social-welfare entitlements and travel and meal allowances are also paid. The programme has been aided by the European Social Fund since its inception in 1989 and now offers 5 000 places per annum. In 1997, 73 per cent of graduates progressed to employment or further education or training (see project description).

"VTOS [the Vocational Training Opportunities Scheme] has had a huge impact on building up my self-esteem. As sentient beings it is only natural that we would aspire to something of a higher level than being on the dole" (the comment of an unemployed man).

"The assumption is that offering a rich variety of educational experiences will motivate students to remain in the system."

STUDY SITES

Case study No. 1

> *Project*:   **The Leaving Certificate Applied**
>
> *Starting date*:   1995
>
> **This relatively new qualification appears to have boosted the motivation levels of 16 to 18-year-olds who are not suited to the more academic Leaving Certificate programme**

The Leaving Certificate is ingrained into the national psyche in Ireland. A "good Leaving" is the hope of most parents for their children. But as increasing numbers of young people remained in secondary schools it became obvious that many were not motivated by the traditional two-year academic programme. Alternative programmes were experimented with and, while innovative, they faced the difficulty of achieving the same national status as the Leaving Certificate. Eventually, it was decided to have a new programme under the umbrella of the Leaving Certificate, to be called the Leaving Certificate Applied (LCA).

A strong promotion was needed from the beginning and a business leader was invited to chair the working party that drew up the new curriculum. Its establishment coincided with a growing Irish interest in the work of Howard Gardner on Multiple Intelligences and the challenges posed by his views for devising curricula and assessing students' achievements. His theory moves away from the traditional emphasis within education on a narrow band of linguistic, mathematical and cognitive skills towards an approach which recognises seven broad spheres of intelligence – linguistic, mathematical/cognitive, spatial, musical, bodily/kinaesthetic, interpersonal and intrapersonal. It encourages teachers to identify the ways in which a child is intelligent and to help the child use his/her intelligence to become an effective learner.

The LCA is built around three main strands:

- General education, which includes the areas of modern languages, social education, arts and culture, leisure and recreation.

- Vocational education, which includes mathematics, technology, tourism/catering, horticulture and information technology.

- Vocational preparation and guidance, which also include communication skills and media education.

A key component is the way in which students are assessed and examined. Students accumulate up to 100 credits during a two-year programme. A student receives one credit for satisfactorily completing a module ("Satisfactory completion" requires students to attend at least 90 per cent of the sessions). Since students take 40 modules, they can gain 40 credits for completing them. Final examinations

115|

account for 33 credits; external examinations are set in five areas – English and Communication; Two Vocational Specialities; Mathematical Applications; Irish and Modern European Languages; Social Education. The remaining 27 credits are distributed according to criteria used in assessing student tasks – practical activities or projects in which students working individually or in teams apply their classroom experiences to "real" situations. The tasks are graded by external assessors who interview the students.

The LCA is offered in more than 200 schools and centres, alongside the established Leaving Certificate. One such school is in Ballyphehane in Cork where the Presentation Order of nuns has a secondary school catering for 400 pupils from a broad socio-economic background. The school has disadvantaged status, which entitles it to additional funding and staffing. Up to 80 per cent of the students in the Leaving Certificate Applied Class whom we met work part-time in local businesses. The school recognises the need to "push" the academically bright on the established Leaving Certificate programme while offering valuable educational experiences to those on the LCA. This is in line with its philosophy of catering for the needs of individual pupils. It is also important in the context of declining enrolments and competition between schools.

Ballyphehane has a long tradition of involvement in curricular innovations, so the introduction of the LCA in 1997 was less of a shock than it might have been to other schools. Its first batch of LCA "graduates" pursued various career and education paths after leaving the school in 1998. More than a third went on to a local further education college, mainly to take secretarial courses. Virtually all the others went directly into employment. Even without the economic boom, the recruitment rate would probably have been good because employers were pleased with the programme and offered jobs to work-experience students. The four periods of work-experience over the two years allow the participants opportunities to try a variety of jobs.

The experiences gained from the student tasks are also important, in particular the benefits of working as a team on a class project. In Cork, one group did a presentation on the film *Titanic* that it staged for another class. The participants all undertook different duties, from preparing invitations on the computer and printing them to introducing the presentation to the guests. All found it worthwhile and regarded it as an achievement.

Two other outcomes warrant mention. The first is the healthy self-esteem among the participants which was evident during the OECD visit. They did not have any sense of failure for not having attempted the established Leaving Certificate programme but rather a sense of achievement for tackling the LCA.

The other welcome outcome is the students' commitment to further education or training as the basis of lifelong learning. Students can participate in further education courses which have mushroomed in the past decade and which are validated by the National Council for Vocational Awards. They can then go on to study for higher education qualifications. The increasing availability of part-time further education opportunities will make that progression easier in future.

Case study No. 2

Project:	**YOUTHREACH**
Starting date:	1988

More than 100 centres are now offering this programme which is transforming the lives of some of Ireland's least-advantaged school-leavers

YOUTHREACH is the main official response to the challenge of motivating young people who have left school with minimal or no qualifications and who are over 15. Conventional schooling left many of the participants with a sense of uselessness and failure; they have short-term goals and unrealistic ambitions; they are also mistrustful of the "system" and may have been in trouble with the law. The author of an evaluation report consulted YOUTHREACH participants and found that:

"The most significant recurring themes were responsibility, trust, choice and respect. For many of the young people involved, YOUTHREACH represents the first environment in which anyone has taken time to listen to them. In some centres, young people contract themselves into the programmes, are consulted on rules and rule changes and are responsible for centre upkeep and hygiene. A participative rather than didactic methodology is applied in general. Persons are generally persuaded rather than forced into situations (ESF Evaluation Unit, 1996)."

The diversity and richness of the experiences and programmes available in the 100 centres is also unusual. For instance, the Hi-w@y internet café in the town of Navan focuses on disadvantaged early school-leavers at risk of exclusion in a knowledge society. It is an innovative response to the challenges of integrating new technology into the informal education sector. The venture is part-funded by the EU programme, Youthstart, and partners from three centres in Germany have participated in an exchange visit to Navan, developing friendships which have continued through e-mail contact.

The centre has transformed the lives of many of the participants, giving them secretarial and information technology (IT) skills that are in demand by employers in the bustling Co Meath town. Three of the female participants were studying to become IT teachers and pass on their new skills to other trainees and to local schools. The centre also functions as a *café* for the general public, serving snacks and light meals. The tasks of preparing the food and serving the customers are shared by the participants. Coming into contact with the public gives them

117|

self-confidence, especially when adults ask for help with sending e-mail messages to family members abroad. The trainees get an allowance and refer to their "job" in YOUTHREACH rather than to training or education.

In nearby Drogheda, the YOUTHREACH centre shares a large building in the middle of town with a number of small businesses. Virtually all the young people involved have negative feelings about formal schooling, but this centre is a hive of activity. It focuses on the holistic development of the individual and provides a safe learning environment. This is particularly important, given that some of them have serious personal problems relating to crime/drug abuse/poverty.

The centre has its own drama group, and it has made two short films, one of which, "Rebels", was screened on national television. The participants have also built their own boats, including an 18 foot "Celtic Warrior" which is used as a rowing/sailing skiff. Their samba workshops are very popular and they organise exhibitions of their work, including one on attitudes towards discrimination. The overall programme focuses on the preparation of young people for their career. The module on enterprise is therefore extremely relevant. The three groups that are based in the centre are involved in very different enterprises – a sandwich service, and the production of greeting cards and stained-glass mirrors. The greeting cards project featured in the final of a local enterprise competition. The sheer variety of successful activities creates its own "feel-good" factor for the trainees who develop a sense of belonging to a programme that works.

Apart from the dedication of the staff and the support of the county's Vocational Education Committee, two other features stand out. One is the links with outside bodies, both locally and cross-border. These links are an essential part of the process of developing good referral and progression routes for participants. The other is the flexibility over funding. In the Drogheda case, other sources were tapped, such as the Special Support Programme for Peace and Reconciliation. This allowed the organisers to buy in additional services to provide a richer educational environment for the participants. The educational approach is challenging; it accepts where each young person is starting from, helping him/her to map out a route. The centre offers a different menu to the traditional school but the outcomes are comparable.

Case study No. 3

Project: **Vocational Training Opportunities Scheme (VTOS)**

Starting date: 1989

The long-term unemployed are being given the opportunity to return to education and learn how to use state-of-the-art IT and video equipment

Galway is a thriving city, one of the fastest-growing in Europe. It is the cultural capital of the west of Ireland, a busy tourist resort and home to many of the new industries that have fuelled Ireland's economic boom. Alongside expensive housing and hotels, however, it has pockets of serious disadvantage, marked by low educational achievement.

The city's Vocational Education Committee, in partnership with local agencies and statutory bodies, offers a range of full-time courses designed to meet the needs of both clients and the local economy. One or two-year courses are offered in: business and marketing; community and health services; computer and environmental studies; design technology; general studies; interior design; languages and business studies; media studies; sound engineering; television and video production; and the established Leaving Certificate. The general studies courses are mainly aimed at those who need a basic foundation level programme, while most of the others are further education courses. Participants receive a training allowance in lieu of a social welfare payment, plus a modest meal allowance. Some are also entitled to fuel and butter vouchers, rent and/or travel allowances.

The programme options are offered under the broad heading of VTOS. They are available in two centres which cater for 240 participants ranging in age from their early twenties to over 60. About 30-40 participants are non-nationals. Between them, the centres have 28 mainly part-time teachers as well as other co-ordinating and administrative staff.

The centres have state-of-the-art equipment, especially in the information technology and video-production areas. That fact, coupled with the possibilities of progression to higher education, has attracted participants who, while unemployed and eligible, are not seriously disadvantaged, perhaps having completed lower or upper secondary education. It is worth noting, however, that the eligibility criteria for VTOS have been widened considerably since its introduction in 1989. The qualifying period was reduced from 12 months' unemployment to six months in 1994. This significantly increased the potential target group.

Getting to the long-term unemployed is, of course, extremely challenging. VTOS has been a successful programme: indeed, its very success is one of the reasons it has become "respectable" and attracted middle-class clientele. However,

119|

its national co-ordinator is conscious of the dangers of it being "colonised" by the more advantaged unemployed who already have an upper secondary education. Partly at her suggestion, a review is under way on how it can also reach the most marginalised and encourage them back into learning.

A report from the European Social Fund Evaluation Unit has recommended the introduction of separate criteria for different levels of VTOS. The unit suggested that eligibility for the foundation level be reduced to one week and raised to one year for further education courses (ESF Evaluation Unit, 1998). In Galway the organisers have made great efforts to attract the seriously disadvantaged through leaflet distribution, church announcements, setting up desks in social welfare offices, developing links with other training-providers and employment services, and using past participants to encourage others to join. The organisers also arranged for a local radio station to broadcast a popular three-hour show from one of the VTOS centres. Their efforts have been rewarded but they accept that it is an on-going struggle to persuade the seriously disadvantaged to take that first step through the door of the centre. Once inside, they are happy to stay. As two brothers on the Galway course remarked: "It's the best thing that ever happened to us."

The Evaluation Unit and the government's recent Green Paper on adult education had also recommended the introduction of part-time and flexible VTOS courses. A further recommendation for better guidance-counselling services for VTOS participants highlights one area that needs addressing.

* * *

Innovation and effectiveness

The rich variety of educational initiatives in Ireland offers valuable insights into the profession of teaching and many are excellent models. The features that seem to work in motivating groups and individuals who did not relate well to traditional schooling include:

- Curricular innovation which is person-centred rather than subject-centred.
- Different forms of assessment.
- Teamwork combined with a willingness to change the core team of teachers involved when necessary.
- Links which harness practical community support in terms of recognition, resources and work-placements.
- Good relationships between teachers and students.

- The use of information technologies in informal education settings.

- Enterprise/work-experience elements.

- Flexibility of funding.

Surveys point to the national success of the three programmes described in this chapter. Progression rates into employment, further education or training are very high and relatively easy to monitor. Harder to quantify are the personal benefits such as higher self-esteem and improved motivation, as well as the benefits to society in terms of savings on social security and health costs for those who could have drifted into long-term unemployment.

Transferability of strategies

The three programmes have a number of elements that can be applied elsewhere. There are no "typical" YOUTHREACH, Leaving Certificate Applied or VTOS students and the programmes start from where the clients are rather than where they should be. They are all *learner-centred* and this involves believing that the students possess knowledge, skills and know-how. The three programmes involve experiential, action-orientated learning.

Although both VTOS and YOUTHREACH are national programmes *the localisation of management* allows for greater flexibility in meeting the diverse needs of potential participants. Modularisation, part-time and weekend-opportunities are being developed. As the YOUTHREACH national co-ordinator, Dermot Stokes, comments: "Localisation of management allows for the education and training to be contoured according to the local educational, economic and cultural landscape." Surveys have shown just how diverse and acute those local needs can be. Around 30 per cent of YOUTHREACH participants have spent less than one year in secondary school, and/or have "difficult domestic/community circumstances" and/or were abusing alcohol or other substances.

The importance attached to *Information and Communication Technologies* (ICTs) in all the programmes cannot be overstated. ICTs can transform the learning situation, giving the learner greater control over the pace of acquiring new knowledge and skills, and altering the relationship between the "teacher" and the "student". Computer literacy is seen by education and training-providers as essential if disadvantaged people are not to be left further behind in the Information Society.

Equally important is the need for *support services* for students. Attracting the most marginalised into a learning environment is one challenge, retaining them is another. There is a particular need for personal and vocational guidance, and access to specialist support. The networking between the school/centre and the wider community provides opportunities for developing contacts with other individuals and agencies that can also provide support.

121

Adequate resources and national certification are obvious requirements for any successful programme as well as properly structured *in-service development* of staff. Teachers and trainers need to have a variety of skills if they are to relate to their students in a manner different from the traditional, subject-based secondary teacher. Teaching in Ireland, as in other OECD countries, is becoming a "greying profession" and many older teachers find it difficult to countenance the changes in approach that will be required if this new client group is to get the attention it needs.

Commentary

The department's policy focuses on the development of a continuum from pre-school through to adult education but there is still some way to go towards reaching that goal. The various initiatives have developed in a patchwork manner as policies evolved and resources became available and there is need for a greater co-ordination of effort between them. There is also need for on-going evaluation but it is recognised that some programmes are so recent that it is difficult to gauge their effectiveness at this stage. However, some attempt might be made to assess the quality of work-placements from programmes such as YOUTHREACH and VTOS.

Undoubtedly, the shortage of staff for many industries makes it somewhat easier to place disadvantaged people in work. It has arrested the drift towards "qualifications inflation" which had characterised employment patterns in Ireland up to the early 1990s when employers were able to draw from a pool of over-qualified people competing for limited openings. Shortages alone, however, will not compel employers to take on people who lack the necessary basic skills: indeed, some Irish employers are already recruiting overseas to fill vacancies in the teleservices, software and catering industries.

Overall, it is clear that early school-leaving and lack of motivation are problems in Ireland as they are in almost every other country. A recent study carried out for the City of Dublin Vocational Education Committee found that just over two-thirds of young school-leavers appeared to have become alienated from school (O'Sullivan, 1999). More of the same in traditional secondary school settings is not the answer for those "failed" by the education system. There is an alternative approach embedded in the three programmes described in this chapter – of affirmative but challenging education, with the person and the process of development at the centre, rather than the subject.

Bibliography

DEPARTMENT OF EDUCATION AND SCIENCE (1998),
"Adult Education in an Era of Lifelong Learning", Dublin.

ESF EVALUATION UNIT (1996),
Evaluation Report: Early School Leavers Provision, European Social Fund Evaluation Unit, Dublin.

EUROPEAN SOCIAL FUND EVALUATION UNIT (1998),
"Evaluation Report, ESF and the Long Term Unemployed", Dublin.

NATIONAL ECONOMIC AND SOCIAL FORUM (1997),
"Early School Leavers and Youth Unemployment", *Forum Report No. 11*, January.

O'SULLIVAN, L. (1999),
"Early school leaving in Dublin city", Department of Education and Science, internal document.

SMYTH, E. (1999),
Do Schools Differ?, ESRI, Dublin.

JAPAN

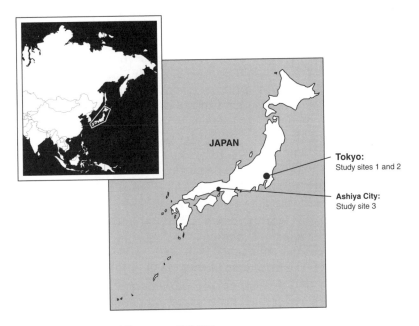

JAPAN

Tokyo:
Study sites 1 and 2

Ashiya City:
Study site 3

Land area in square kilometers: 378 000.

Total population (1998): 126 486 000.

Youth population – under 15 years (1998):
- 19 099 386,
- percentage of total population: 15.1%.

Youth unemployment (1998):
- 15-24 year-olds: 7.7%.

Percentage of 18-year-olds in education.*

Per capita GDP (1997 prices): 24 574 USD.

Birth rate per 1 000 population (1996): 9.5.

* Figures not available.
Sources: Labour Force Statistics: 1979-1998, OECD, Paris; *Annual National Accounts, Main Aggregates, Volume 1, 1999,* OECD, Paris; *Education at a Glance,* OECD Database 1999, Paris.

Country context

Education: The Japanese public school system has two compulsory stages for students aged 6-15: elementary (six years) and lower secondary (three years). Following competitive examinations, most students enter upper secondary education where the majority takes general courses designed for university entry. The Ministry of Education, Science, Sports and Culture (Monbusho) has responsibility for all education from kindergartens to universities, including a substantial and influential private education sector. Monbusho co-operates with the 47 prefectures, each of which has a board of education that acts as a regional education authority. Within the prefectures there are municipalities that also have educational functions. Monbusho has defined a national course of study, for elementary and secondary schools and it also approves school textbooks. While the course of study sets national standards for school curricula, schools may design their own curricula to match local circumstances. Over 40 per cent of high school graduates gain higher education places; about 47 per cent of females and 35 per cent of males. However, more than half of the female students go on to the two-year junior colleges, while close to 95 per cent of the males enter university.

Economy: In the 1980s Japan epitomised the Asian tiger economies with highly successful and sophisticated industrial and financial sectors. The 1990s have seen a major downturn in the economy coinciding with an increasing awareness that fundamental changes have also been occurring in Japanese society. The economic bubble burst in 1993 with an increase in unemployment that was especially marked among women and the youngest and oldest age groups. An OECD report published in 1998 called for the reform of the financial sector, more support for economic activity and reform of the industrial structure. Demographically, there has been a substantial expansion in the size of cities leading to congestion, commuting and the loss of a sense of community. Falling birth rates combined with an aging population have direct implications both for the educational system and social welfare arrangements.

Student motivation issues

Given the very high proportion of Japanese students who enter higher education it might appear that motivation is not a critical issue. Furthermore, Japanese school students have performed very well in international tests. The government is, however, concerned about the figures for truancy, dropouts and anti-social behaviour. It is also worried that the school examinations system may reward the accumulation of factual knowledge rather than the development of skills that will be useful in adult life.

According to a survey by Monbusho, the Ministry of Education, the number of students *truanting* from public and private elementary and lower secondary schools for 30 days or more a year is increasing. In 1997, 21 000 elementary school children and 85 000 lower secondary students were classed as truants (the equivalent figures for 1995 were 17 000 and 65 000). More than four in ten lower secondary truants (42 per cent) said that their absence stemmed from problems with other students and poor examination results; 33 per cent blamed their mental state; and 17 per cent cited problems at home, including relationships with parents.

While the proportion of upper secondary dropouts is not that high compared to other countries, it is considered to be a serious problem. Education is highly valued in Japan and parents expect their children to excel academically and proceed to higher levels. This inevitably discourages dropping out. The fact that the education system makes it difficult for dropouts to resume their studies at a later date also means that students have little choice but to stay in school regardless of their level of motivation.

Monbusho has reported that the percentage of dropouts from public and private upper secondary schools peaked in 1997 at 2.6 per cent (111 000 students) of whom the majority was first-year students (54.8 per cent). Most students dropped out to enter employment or to transfer to other schools, but others left because they had enrolled in upper secondary school without clear objectives and were dissatisfied with their courses and the teaching methods.

Although there is a continuing reference to bullying and school violence in government publications concerned with lifelong learning, surveys reported by Monbusho (1994) suggest that bullying reached a peak in the mid-1980s and has since declined. However, a study published by the Bureau for Youth Problems indicates that the problem has shifted from overt violence to psychological intimidation, such as ostracism (Kajita, 1997). As we shall show later, an extremely violent incident involving school students can have a powerful impact locally and nationally. Such incidents alter the perception of the problem as depicted in national statistics.

To keep the concern for truancy, dropping out and anti-social behaviour in perspective, we need to bear in mind that another Monbusho survey showed that in 1994 some 94 per cent of lower secondary students and 93 per cent of upper secondary students were satisfied with their school life. However, upper secondary students said that their principal sources of dissatisfaction were the "content and process" of teaching, teachers, and their grades.

This concern with grades relates to the highly competitive nature of schooling at all levels in Japan. Competition, seen through the eyes of the winners, can be highly motivating, but for the losers the reverse is true. In fact, there is a marked polarisation among the student population: one group is highly motivated and competitive, but others have little interest in learning. Many members of the latter group are taking part-time jobs, not out of necessity but in order to purchase consumer goods or finance their leisure activities.

There is severe competition in entrance examinations to enter high-status upper secondary schools and universities. This helps to explain why more than a quarter of applicants for higher education are *ronin* – those who have spent at least an extra year on preparatory studies after graduating from upper secondary school. But in large cities, even elementary school children are obliged to compete for places in desirable lower secondary schools. This competition has led to increases in the proportion of elementary and lower secondary students attending private tutoring schools or *juku* (Monbusho, 1994), which supplement the teaching they receive during the day. In some city areas, it would not be unusual for a lower secondary student to attend juku or other classes for sport and other activities until 10 p.m or even later every weekday and even on the weekend. This situation is tolerated because it has been generally believed – at least up until the current economic downturn – that by winning a place at a renowned university a student can secure a good job for life. Because of the discriminatory recruitment policies adopted by many Japanese employers this has been especially true for male students.

Students we met were not unhappy with their *juku* classes. Indeed, some preferred them to their normal school lessons. This was partly because there was a choice of classes – especially in the urban areas – but also because the *juku* enabled them to meet friends and establish closer links with teachers than in their normal schools. However, there was competition to register for the best juku, and there was usually a strict testing regime in these schools.

Juku is a feature of all levels of education from kindergartens to universities. These tutoring schools act as a powerful force that has to be taken into account when educational reforms in the public sector are being formulated. Monbusho has expressed concern that excessive *juku* attendance limits children's opportunities for play and other everyday experiences that are appropriate to their stage of development. Correcting this enormous concentration on examination success has been one of the major issues facing Japanese education. It is recognised that reform is needed but it will not be easy to achieve because conventional examinations have arguably become even more important since the economic downturn of 1993. Schools will, however, have to do more to prepare students for the economic and social changes that they are likely to encounter in adult life.

Because of the new economic climate, even blue-chip companies are much less likely to offer a job for life and unemployment rates for 16 to 25-year-olds, particularly for women, have been increasing. However, the strong attachment of parents and teachers to high-status schools and universities is a formidable barrier to change. Indeed, the social status of Japanese graduates – as well as their employment prospects – is largely dependent on the ranking of the university they attended. All state schools and private schools are also ranked and it is the determination to get as far up the pecking order as possible that motivates teachers and students at all levels of education.

Main policy approaches

While it is possible to trace Japanese government interest in lifelong learning to the 1970s, the enactment in 1990 of the Law for Promoting Lifelong Learning was an important milestone. This prompted the setting up of the National Council for Lifelong Learning that has produced a series of advisory reports on issues such as strengthening the links between schools and their communities.

Consultative bodies are highly important in the Japanese political system: they help to prepare policy proposals and also evaluate new initiatives. In 1996, another of these bodies, the Central Council for Education (1996), proposed the encouragement of a "zest for living" (*ikuru chikara*):

"It was clear to us that what our children will need in future, regardless of the way in which society changes, are the qualities and the ability to identify problem areas for themselves, to learn, think, make judgements and act independently and to be more adept at problem-solving. We also felt that they need to be imbued with a rich sense of humanity in the sense that while exercising self-control, they must be able to co-operate with others, have consideration for their needs and have a spirit that feels emotion. It also goes without saying that if they are to lead vigorous lives, a healthy body is an indispensable requirement. We decided to use the term *zest for living* to describe the qualities and abilities needed to live in a period of turbulent change and felt it is important to encourage the right balance between the separate factors underlying this term."

This statement, with its sharp focus on the learner, has implications for the organisation of the school curriculum and timetable, for teaching and learning strategies and for student assessment. It reinforces the proposals made by the Curriculum Council in 1987 for new courses of study to be based on respect for the individual. The term "scholastic ability" was introduced to cover such aspects as students' willingness to learn independently and the ability to think, judge and express themselves. Monbusho argued that what was required was a major modification in the ways in which "educators and the general public think about education and evaluate children" (Monbusho, 1994).

In order to develop the zest for living, the Curriculum Council said it was vital to

- Teach subjects in a way that motivates students to study and learn.
- Enhance problem-solving and learning through experience and increase students' study choices to respect their individuality.
- Introduce teaching methods responsive to the needs of individual students.

In 1998, the council reduced the number of class hours and the content of the curriculum to provide space for promoting the "zest for living". Standards are now more generalised and flexible and schools are expected to create their own curricula reflecting local circumstances. There has also been an increase in the number of elective subjects at lower secondary school. This is also intended to motivate students.

Three other developments are linked to these proposals for the reduction of curriculum pressure. The first is the staged introduction since 1992 of the five school-days-per-week scheme so that there will be no half-day schooling on Saturdays after 2002. The second is the promotion of the "Period for Integrated Studies" at all levels of schooling and the third, and most recent (1999), is the unification of lower secondary and upper secondary schools (see Case study 2).

There has also been an increasing interest in the role of families in school education. Clearly, many parents invest heavily both in private schooling and in *juku* – particularly at the lower secondary stage. One survey of 150 schools that was carried out for Monbusho in 1996-97 suggested that 75 per cent of state school lower secondary pupils attended juku or had a home tutor. Their parents spent an average of JPY 215 986 a year (US$1 939) on supplementary education. A smaller proportion of private lower secondary students attended juku (58 per cent), but their parents paid marginally more, on average, for their extra studies (JPY 216 143). However, it is argued that there is much to be gained from closer co-operation between schools, families and local communities, not least in motivating young people to engage in activities other than cramming for examinations (see Case study 3).

While these motivation-related reforms and policies have affected all schools, there are some changes that apply only to upper secondary schools, including:

- Integrated courses, bridging general and vocational studies, where students select subjects suited to their personal interests and create their own curricula guided by teachers. Introduced in 1994, there are now 124 public and private courses of this kind in all but one of the prefectures.

- Credit-system upper secondary schools that allow any individual to receive upper secondary education as part of lifelong learning. These schools, which have been in operation since 1988, are characterised by a curriculum that is not divided into year groups. Students graduate by accumulating the required number of credits. They may enter during any semester and may bring with them credits obtained at another upper secondary school. Credit-system schools offer many subjects and provide classes at various hours, including during Saturdays and Sundays (Case study 1). There are currently 266 public and private credit-system upper secondary schools in all 47 prefectures. About half of them offer full-time courses, the remainders provide night and correspondence courses.

- Alternative methods of selecting students. A growing number of upper secondary schools have introduced new selection policies – interviews, short essays or recommendations from lower secondary schools – to reduce the importance of the entrance examination.

In addition to reforming school organisation and curricula the government has sought to improve career guidance and counselling in schools. The focus at the point of transfer from lower to upper secondary is on school selection. Less attention has been paid to the most appropriate upper secondary pathways for individual students. The government believes that students need more help in understanding the various choices they can make about the future (Monbusho, 1994). But it wants students to make their own decisions and take responsibility for those choices.

"The number of class hours and the curriculum content have been reduced to provide space for promoting a 'zest for living'."

"Students at Shinjuku Yamabuki school can attend classes on a day and time convenient to them."

131

STUDY SITES

Case study No. 1

Institution:	**Shinjuku Yamabuki Upper Secondary School**
Location:	**Tokyo**
Starting date:	**1991**

Former truants and dropouts are being offered a second chance at an upper secondary school that operates an unusual shift system

The opening of the Shinjuku Yamabuki Upper Secondary School coincided with the release of a 1991 report (Central Council for Education, 1991) proposing various reforms to upper secondary education. It recommended the establishment of a credit-based system where the curriculum is not structured by year grades. Under this arrangement, students may graduate whenever they have accumulated the required number of credits. Students following part-time courses and correspondence courses have benefited from such a system since 1988. In 1992, it became available to full-day students as well.

The credit system allows students to create their own study plans, enabling them to work independently when necessary. Such plans are likely to reflect their own aptitudes, interests, and career aspirations. It is argued (Monbusho, 1994) that it "should be possible to use the special characteristics of the credit-based system to prevent a decrease in the motivation to learn and the drop-out phenomenon".

The principal of Shinjuku Yamabuki school emphasised that the credit-based system offered students a second chance. It also enabled them to move from one school to another, carrying their credit with them. He was proud that, although students had to compete for places at his school, account was not taken of their previous school experience. Students were not penalised for having been truants or dropouts earlier.

Special courses had been designed for adults though some of them were studying alongside conventional upper secondary students. The school accommodates some 1 300 conventional students and 1 150 recurrent students, who usually attend only one day a week. Half of their credits must come from compulsory courses; the remainder from courses they have chosen themselves after receiving guidance and counselling from the three specialist staff in the school.

Central to the school's programme of studies is a four-shift system offering flexibility to students who may attend classes on a day and time convenient to them. They may attend one of two courses, each of which includes electives, and any of the four shifts. Although the school does not claim to have introduced innovative teaching methods, the principal emphasised that many of the adult students had been truants or dropouts from other schools where they had been dissatisfied with the learning environment. They would be unlikely to tolerate teaching methods not designed in their interests.

The school also provided conventional correspondence courses for those students unable to attend classes for health reasons or because of job or family commitments. About half of the adult students were women.

No formal internal or external evaluation had been undertaken of the strengths and weaknesses of this credit system. There was government recognition that the arrangements were worthy of consideration by others and they had been used as an example in a Monbusho document (Monbusho, 1994). At the time of our visit, plans were in place for an evaluation to mark the school's tenth anniversary.

The principal pointed to the heavy costs of running a complicated, credit-based system. Electives meant smaller classes, even though the general studies classrooms were designed for the conventional classes of 40 students, and more teachers. Managing the timetables for staff was also difficult, not least because the school was open on Saturdays and Sundays, as well as from 8.45 a.m to 9.20 p.m every weekday. He felt that this would discourage prefectures from introducing many credit-based upper secondary schools of this kind. Although, as mentioned earlier, there are 266 credit-based upper secondaries in Japan, few offer the degree of flexibility to be found at Shinjuku Yamabuki school.

Asked about the motivation levels in his school, the principal said that the students' destination statistics provided the best testimony. Although these were second-chance students, 70 per cent of them would go on to university and the remainder would enter vocationally orientated colleges.

Case study No. 2

Institution: **Attached Secondary School to the University of Tokyo**
Project starting date: 1963

This experimental school asks prospective students to take an entrance test but it believes that there is more to education than preparing for examinations

Established in 1948 during the American occupation, this school was intended to fulfil three functions: to introduce innovative practices; to avoid elitism; and to provide slow learners with special education, including vocational training. In effect, the school has focused on the first two aims and has made a special feature of educating twins.

The school recruits students using a mixture of lottery and scholastic ability examinations from all parts of Tokyo. From the outset it has been a combined

133|

lower and upper secondary school with automatic transfer between the two sec
tors. As such, it clearly preceded the proposals for consistent education contained
in the 1998 amendment to the School Education Law. As long ago as 1963 it had
introduced a 2-2-2 arrangement in which the first two years of secondary schooling
are considered to be foundation years, followed by two reinforcing years, termi
nating with two advanced or developmental years. The school was proud of its cur
riculum that had been designed to meet the minimum national requirements for
class hours and credits but also had a unique elective subject arrangement. The
school administrators pointed out that their students do not have automatic
access to the University of Tokyo. However, in many attached schools in Japan, stu
dents can move on to higher levels in the same school without open competition
in some cases even from kindergarten to graduate school. This means that the
competition for places in some prestigious institutions is pushed down to the
lower age groups.

During our visit the deputy principal explained that, since 1981, students have
been put into groups of four or five members on entry to the school. Each group
meets once a week for two hours to take part in largely self-determined learning
activities. 1981 also saw the introduction of thematic, or integrated, studies that
bridged the final year of lower secondary education and the first year of upper
secondary education. Teachers provide students with a list of themes from which
they select those they wish to study. Although the choice has to be made by the
group this is seen as a way to stimulate students' personal interests and channel
their curiosity. The themes are drawn from real-life issues giving the students the
opportunity to share their reflections with other group members and classes and
enabling them to acquire report writing and presentational skills that will be useful in later studies, especially in universities.

Some of these features were highlighted in a lesson we observed in a school
hall where three lower secondary classes, approximately 120 students, were
arranged in large groups. They were studying an environmental theme: using
detailed street maps they had located trees in their home neighbourhoods and
were assessing their health. All the students were undertaking the same task
directed by a worksheet and a teacher who addressed them by microphone. He
was supported by other teachers who moved between the groups offering help
and encouragement as needed. The exercise concluded with pairs of students
giving oral, illustrated presentations of their findings to all the students.

Here were aspects of group activities, peer support, team teaching, integrated
studies and thematic enquiry that find echoes in Monbusho reports. The school
was making a deliberate attempt to introduce a learning environment that was
different from the preparation for tests and examinations.

This emphasis on skills and integrated studies in which the students take responsibility for what and how to study was also evident in what were referred to as 'graduation projects". Towards the end of the lower secondary school, students were asked to prepare a project report on a topic of their choice that would be submitted at the end of upper secondary school. We looked at two of these projects, one an empirical study of memory and the other a technical study of robotics. These were well presented and detailed studies that demonstrated the students' enthusiasm for individualised study. The students received personalised tutorial support and their work was displayed to parents and others at an open day. The deputy principal believed these projects were highly motivating and enabled the students to acquire skills that would be useful in university or in adult life.

The group activities and independent studies are in harmony with government proposals associated with the zest for living. What was not clear was the interaction between these innovations and the mainstream curriculum. One student we interviewed said that he was torn between subject learning which led to entrance exams and group activities which he enjoyed but could not afford to spend too much time on. It may also be significant that this innovative work does not appear to have been copied by other schools.

Case study No. 3

Location: **Ashiya City in the Hyogo Prefecture, southwest Japan**

Project starting date: **1998**

The after-shocks from a devastating earthquake and a highly-publicised murder have caused the Hyogo prefecture to reconsider the demands that secondary schooling makes on students

This project enables lower secondary students to spend a week in which they "can do and try whatever they want to do". The project title, Trai-yaru Week contains a pun that not only draws attention to the need to try new things but refers to the "tri", as in triangle. This highlights the tripartite partnership between school, family and local community.

The week of out-of-school activity has been offered to 14-year-olds since April 1998. Many interlocking reasons were given for this innovation:

- The Great Hanshin-Awaji Earthquake on January 17, 1995, devastated the local community and caused its members to think harder about such issues as respect for nature, the dignity of human life, community co-operation and the potential of volunteers in schools.
- A brutal murder in which a teenager beheaded a younger child in Kobe city in the Hyogo prefecture had focused people's minds on social harmony; violence

135|

in schools was also increasing and more young people were becoming delinquent.

- Between the ages of 13 and 15, students' emotional and physical growth causes them to be confused about the present and uneasy about the future.

- The school curriculum and organisation were perceived as rigid and uniform.

- Family relations were deteriorating in response to: parents' changing working conditions (long hours and the movement of fathers to workplaces distant from home); the over-protective attitude of parents, and the impact of new technology (mass media and computers) that reduced the quality of family relationships.

- Too much weight was placed by parents on entrance examinations to high-status schools, colleges and universities and this meant that schools could not allocate time to students' personal and social education.

- Teachers had difficulty in introducing elective subjects and matching the pupils' interests with the curriculum.

In July 1997, the Hyogo Prefectural Board of Education held an emergency meeting at which the following proposal was discussed:

"It is necessary to shift the emphasis from an education where we have tried to teach lots of knowledge for results to one where we support students to learn to acquire a way of living or a zeal for living."

Plans were drawn up to help students increase their creativity and sensitivity and to find their ideal lifestyles by providing them with sufficient time and space. It was also agreed to engage three partners – school, family and local community – in preparing and promoting an innovative scheme.

The *trai-yaru* week was made available for all second-year students in the 359 public lower secondary schools in Hyogo prefecture. Approximately 59 000 students participated in the scheme in 1999, supported by some 23 000 volunteers.

Most schools organised the *trai-yaru* weeks during the month of June, because it was hoped that lessons learned during the week would influence students' behaviour during the summer vacation. The activities can be grouped under five headings, and the percentage of students involved in the activities in 1998 are shown in brackets.

- *Work experience in service occupations: e.g.* supermarket, post office, restaurant (72 per cent).

- *Other work:* dairy farming, fishing, forestry (5 per cent).

- *Welfare activities:* institutions for the old or handicapped, kindergartens (8 per cent).

- *Volunteer activities*: visiting victims of the earthquake and environmental surveys (7 per cent).

- *Creative activities in culture or art*: ceramics, tea ceremony, flower arranging (6 per cent).

The great majority of students (88 per cent) were able to take part in their first or second-choice activity. During the visit to the Hyogo prefecture we were able to observe and meet small groups of students from Yamate Junior Secondary School in Ashiya, which is one of the most affluent cities in Japan. They were supervising children in a kindergarten, helping to care for elderly disabled persons in a nursing home, assisting in a small supermarket, and serving in a fast-food restaurant. Students were enthusiastic about the activities and the opportunity to learn about working life. Although they did not go to the lower secondary school during the *trai-yaru* week they continued to attend *juku* and this placed heavy pressures on them. But there were some unforeseen consolations. One boy said that his mother had never come to his school but she had visited the supermarket to see him at work.

No formal evaluation of this project had been commissioned but the Hyogo Prefectural Board of Education had made some preliminary judgements regarding outcomes for students, parents, the community and the schools. It was claimed that some students had come to know themselves better from making contacts with people in the local area. Some had learned about what was important in working life, contrasting this reality with what they encountered at school and at home. Others had learned about the discipline of working life and also about the importance of relating well to adults.

Parents reported that they had spent more time talking with their children since the scheme began and others commented that it had caused them to reflect on the best way to raise children. Local residents, in turn, said that the image of students had been changed for the better.

Teachers were also challenged to think more about educational reforms and to reflect on the importance of learning through activities in local communities. As part of the scheme, teachers were expected to visit the students during the *trai-yaru* week and to discuss their experiences with the activity organisers. However, no special in-service training was provided for teachers to help them to maximise the learning experiences of the students and it appeared that no time had been made available to follow up the students' experiences when they returned to school after the *trai-yaru* week.

* * *

Innovation and effectiveness

There can be no doubting the importance attached by Monbusho to lifelong learning. The Ministry recognises that schools must prepare students for a future of increasing uncertainty.

However, the Japanese educational system remains rigidly structured and heavily focused on knowledge accumulation through memorising and one-way teaching. Preparation for entrance examinations overwhelms all other educational activities. As we have pointed out, uncertainty about the future, especially the threat of unemployment, could intensify the competition for places in high-status educational institutions. It could also be a launch pad for reform initiatives. At this juncture, it appears that the old and new education agendas are in competition. For instance, Monbusho proposals to reduce curriculum content, introduce electives, change teaching methods and examinations, and give students more responsibility for decisions regarding their own education, can be countered by parents who may invest more in private cramming lessons for their offspring.

Nevertheless, there is evidence in Monbusho reports and from what we were able to observe during our visit that schools are able to innovate in order to provide greater motivation for their students. The three Japanese study sites demonstrate that schools can give teenagers opportunities to choose studies that engage them as individuals. It is also evident that space can be found in timetables for new methods of teaching, such as group work and team teaching, and that arrangements can be made for students to take part in out-of-school learning activities that contribute to direct family and community involvement in education.

Interestingly, the innovations in Case studies 1 and 2 preceded government proposals for more widespread adoption. Indeed, in Case study 2 the changes have been long established and have offered the government examples of practice for others to consider.

In the absence of formal internal or external evaluations of these innovations it is difficult to determine their effectiveness. The highlighting of specific school innovations in government publications indicates that these are models worth considering in other prefectures. But formal evaluations of the effectiveness of the innovations would contribute to their dissemination. Such evaluations might also provide some understanding of how the innovations have affected examination performance and the teaching of conventional subjects. Are the innovations the key to curricular reform or are they on the margins of the mainstream curriculum? Do they motivate students to study in different ways and, if so, what is the carry-over from the innovations to other learning contexts? Further, how do the innovations contribute to a zest for living that continues beyond the upper secondary school into further studies or employment? Importantly, what are the incentives for schools and teachers to engage in innovations that, inevitably, carry a risk factor and might be seen to threaten examination success? Finally, to what extent are any of the innovations limited by a lack of appropriate teacher training?

Transferability

As we have indicated, the credit-based scheme at Shinjuku Yamabuki Upper Secondary had features that limited its transferability. For example, substantial costs were incurred in offering an elective system based on a shift arrangement. Nevertheless, 266 schools across Japan are now using a credit-based system. They offer opportunities for students who would otherwise have been unable to graduate with upper secondary qualifications. However, to what extent their qualifications are recognised in society in general and the labour market in particular remains to be seen. Until recently, qualifications obtained through alternative routes, such as night high schools and night sections of universities, have not enjoyed the same level of recognition.

There was less evidence of transfer of innovations from the Attached Secondary School (Case study 2). There are a number of attached schools in Japan as well as schools with more than one education levels. They have introduced curriculum changes and other innovations but in many cases these modifications are geared towards entrance-exam preparation.

The third, the *trai-yaru* week, was part of a recent, prefecture-wide initiative involving a large number of students in many schools. Although there were special circumstances in the prefecture that led to the introduction of this out-of-school week, the principles underpinning it, especially the need to provide students with authentic experiences and to link schools with their local communities, are transferable. Indeed, they are prominent in the guidelines on motivating students that Monbusho issues to schools. Other prefectures appear to be interested in introducing similar arrangements, but by last summer the *trai-yaru* week had yet to be adopted elsewhere in Japan.

In a broader international context, the development of flexible credit accumulation and transfer systems in upper secondary education is already well advanced in a number of countries, as reported in other chapters of this report. There are also many echoes of the teaching strategies such as group work, team teaching and independent thematic studies to be found in many countries. The *trai-yaru* week, with its strong emphasis on the student's personal and social education and the close involvement of the local community, has features that can be set alongside work-experience programmes in other countries. It is the integration of out-of-school activities into the mainstream curriculum that poses a new challenge for the schools of Hyogo prefecture and the lessons learned in this process are likely to be of interest elsewhere in Japan and beyond.

Commentary

There can be no doubt that Japanese adolescents can be motivated to engage in intensive studies geared towards examination success. Parents are prepared to invest heavily both in private schooling and in *juku* and such parental involvement would be envied in many other countries. What was being challenged before the economic downturn, and has been reinforced by it, is the way that society and the educational system responds to the concept of lifelong learning. To date, the education system has focused almost exclusively on the needs of young learners because the Japanese tend to divide life into the learning stage (up to early adulthood) and the working stage. Adult education has therefore been well down the public policy agenda.). In this context, motivating adolescents towards future learning in leisure, vocational and community contexts with less emphasis on motivation towards examination success is also very difficult.

The innovations described in this chapter have the support of some senior staff in schools, and these grassroots initiatives have contributed to the formulation of government policies. What is not clear is how much teacher training is being provided to support these innovations, and whether there will be any fundamental impact on the Japanese educational system or student learning.

Bibliography

CENTRAL COUNCIL FOR EDUCATION (1991),
   Educational Reforms for the New Era, Tokyo.

CENTRAL COUNCIL FOR EDUCATION (1996),
   The Model for Japanese Education in the Perspective of the Twenty-first Century, Tokyo.

KAJITA, M. (1997),
   "School education as the foundation for lifelong learning", *Research Bulletin of the National Institute for Educational Research*, Vol. 28, pp. 40-56.

MONBUSHO – MINISTRY OF EDUCATION, SCIENCE, SPORTS AND CULTURE (1994),
   "Japanese Government Policies in Education, Science, Sports and Culture 1994", Tokyo.

OECD (1998),
   OECD *Economic Surveys: Japan*, Paris.

KOREA

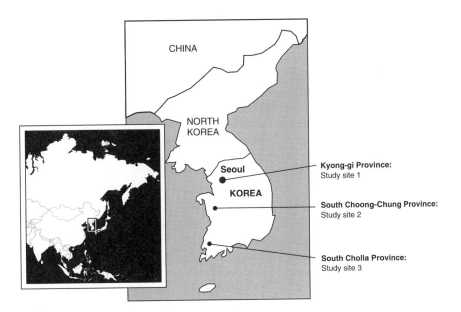

CHINA

NORTH KOREA

Seoul

KOREA

Kyong-gi Province:
Study site 1

South Choong-Chung Province:
Study site 2

South Cholla Province:
Study site 3

Land area in square kilometers: 99 000.

Total population (1998): 46 430 000.

Youth population – under 15 years (1998):
– 10 214 600,
– percentage of total population: 22.0%.

Youth unemployment (1998):
– 15-24 year-olds: 15.9%.

Percentage of 18-year-olds in education (1998): 54%.

Per capita GDP (1997 prices): 14 477 USD.

Birth rate per 1 000 population (1996): 15.2.

Sources: Labour Force Statistics: 1979-1998, OECD, Paris; *Annual National Accounts, Main Aggregates, Volume 1, 1999,* OECD, Paris; *Education at a Glance,* OECD Database 1999, Paris.

Country context

Education: The expansion of Korean education has been as rapid and massive as its economic development since World War Two. The rate of growth at the elementary and middle school levels had slowed by the mid-90s, but the high school and higher education sectors are still expanding. Between 1945 and 1994, school rolls rose from: primary – 1.4 million to 4 million; middle school – 81 000 to 2.5 million; high school – 40 000 to 2.1 million. The number of higher education students also ballooned from 8 000 to 2.2 million (Ministry of Education, 1999). International research has shown that the attainment level of Korean children is very high in maths (OECD, 1998). Almost all middle school graduates enter high school at 16 and over 60 per cent of high school graduates go on to higher education. There is a considerable gender difference in education attainment, though; about two-and-a-half times more males than females have been graduating from university (Ministry of Education, 1998). It is also acknowledged that the rising enrolments have led to overcrowded classrooms, oversized schools and excessive competition in the college entrance examination. As a result, students from affluent families often complete their studies abroad.

Economy: Modern Korean history has been extremely turbulent: North and South Korea remain divided by the Demilitarised Zone (commonly referred to as the DMZ) and many Korean families that were separated by the 1950-53 war have still not been reunited. Monthly defence drills and conscription remain part of Korean life and ongoing tension is inevitable, given that the DMZ is just 55 km north of South Korea's capital, Seoul. Nevertheless, the country has achieved a remarkable economic growth and is now a leading industrialised nation. It was engulfed by the Asian economic crisis two years ago and suffered the worst recession in its postwar history. The latest OECD *Economic Outlook* (1999) commented that "the economy now appears to have bottomed out" but unemployment is likely to remain high at around 7.5 per cent. Before the crisis the jobless rate was as low as 2 per cent. IMF-directed restructuring is now under way.

Student motivation issues

Koreans believe that as the country has very limited natural resources its most important asset is its people. Education is therefore of paramount importance.

The majority of Koreans also believe that education can improve the quality of their lives by enabling them to obtain better jobs and become upwardly mobile (Chin, 1995). This is certainly true for men. However, the proportion of well-educated Korean women who are participating in the labour market is considerably lower than in other countries (OECD, 1998). Women's upward mobility has tended to be accomplished through marriage. Higher education has often been seen as a way of attracting a university-educated husband (Chin, 1995; Lee, 1997).

Korean parents invest heavily in education. It is estimated that they spent more than 9.6 trillion won in 1997 (US$8.06 billion) on private tutoring for their children (Korean Education Development Institute, 1997). This equates to more than half of the Ministry's budget of 18.1 trillion won for the year 1998. The exceptional level of parental investment, coupled with limited higher education opportunities in the past, has helped to create a very competitive education system. Schooling is mainly geared towards university entrance because students' prospects of success in later life are heavily dependent on them winning a place at an elite institution.

The value that Koreans place on education is reflected in a range of statistics that provide some measure of student motivation levels:

- *Drop-out rates*: These are considerably lower than in many other OECD countries, judging by Ministry of Education figures for 1998 – 1.3 per cent in middle school and 2.7 per cent in high school (Ministry of Education, 1998).
- *Higher education aspirations*: One official survey suggested that about 95 per cent of high school students wanted to attain some kind of higher education (Korean Statistical Office, 1997).
- *Achievement level*: No other OECD country matched the maths performance of the Korean fourth and eighth-graders who took part in the Third International Mathematics and Science Study (TIMSS, 1996 and 1997).

Yet students' lack of motivation is recognised as a serious and growing problem. It is now acknowledged that the highly competitive system, which is preoccupied with outcomes (test scores and comparison-based evaluation), fails to motivate many average or below-average students. Low student motivation has, for example, been a major problem in vocational high schools. They make up 40 per cent of Korean high schools and generally cater for those students whose scores are mid- to below-average. Just over a third (36 per cent) of these vocational students proceed to higher education compared to 83 per cent of students in academic high schools (Ministry of Education, 1999).

The almost unparalleled level of parent investment and societal expectation mean that students are under a constant and considerable pressure to stay in the system and excel academically. Korea's rather rigid educational system, which makes it hard to take a break from studies and return at a later date, is an additional

145|

pressure. Therefore, the country's drop-out rate does not necessarily relate to the level of student motivation in Korea.

In fact, many students understandably lose interest in their studies. One Statistical Office survey published in 1997 revealed that only 33 per cent of students were satisfied overall with high school life. Even fewer approved of the curriculum (28 per cent) but almost two-thirds (65 per cent) had satisfactory relationships with other students (Korean Statistical Office, 1997).

The highly competitive system has polarised the country's student population. A minority are keen to succeed, but there are many others who lag behind and are much less motivated. The gap between those two groups seems to widen as students move up from the primary to the secondary level. The TIMSS research found that although there was a relatively even spread of maths attainment among Korean nine-year-olds, by the age of 13 an immense gulf had opened up between the high and low-performers (OECD, 1998; TIMSS, 1996 and 1997).

However, those students who are on the verge of dropping out, as well as those who have already dropped out, get relatively little help and understanding from the education system and their parents. It is recognised that the causes of drop-out are getting more complex and are partly caused by a clash of cultures. As the country has undergone massive changes in a very short period, the generation gap between Korean adults and youths is much wider than in many other countries. Teachers and school administrators tend to be authoritarian and the education system is still characterised by one-way knowledge transmission, universal curriculum and textbooks, and strict school rules. But this form of schooling may be less acceptable to students who are influenced by Western youth culture and consumerism. This paradoxical situation is said to be responsible for an increase in violence, substance abuse, truancy and other behavioural problems. A sharp rise in the rate of juvenile delinquency involving school drop-outs is regarded as an issue that must be tackled immediately.

Main policy approaches

The Seventh Socio-economic Development Plan (1992-96) set Korean educators the goal of producing prospective leaders for the 21st century. The Commission of Education Reform, a consultative body that reports directly to the president, was established in 1993. It introduced two new ideologies: an open education system and a lifelong learning society. These became key concepts for a series of reform plans that aim to create "an open education system and a lifelong learning society in which anyone has a chance to have the education he or she wants for self-realisation, anywhere, anytime (Ministry of Education, 1999)".

The Education Reform Plan of 1996 is significant in fixing clear directions for future policy and switching the emphasis from the providers of education to the receivers; from standardised education to diversified and specialised education; from an educational management system based on regulation and centralised control to one based on responsibility and self-control; from traditional education using blackboards and chalk to one in keeping with the information age; from low-quality to high-quality education by using various performance-based assessment and evaluation instruments.

These ambitious reforms have yet to work their way into the system but fundamental changes in the structure and operation of Korean education are anticipated. This should have a significant impact on student motivation. High schools, for example, can expect:

- *Curriculum*: a switch from a uniform curriculum to a more flexible and autonomous curriculum, the introduction of more elective subjects, and the grouping of students based on their ability levels rather than their grades (year groups).

- *Textbooks*: new books with more practical contents and tailored to students' different ability levels.

- *Teaching and learning methods*: a switch from conventional one-way teaching to students' active involvement in their own learning by using such methods as group learning, hands-on experience, and improved teacher-student ratios.

- *Diversified education*: the setting up or expansion of high schools for students with special talents in maths, science, art and other subjects.

- *Personality development*: to counter the excessive emphasis on academic performance, students' interests and special abilities will be developed through extra-curricular and community service activities.

- *High school and higher education admission*: examination grades will no longer be the sole criterion for selecting students.

The reforms set out in the Non-Formal Education Act of 1982 have been introduced relatively slowly. But the legislation has at least started to address rigidity in the system by creating a variety of flexible learning opportunities for those who were formerly never given a second chance. The following innovations outlined in the act have extended high school students' learning options: air and correspondence high schools; the college-degree-through-self-study programme; industrial universities and night classes affiliated with industrial firms. This act was superseded by the Lifelong Education Act 1999, which came into effect last year.

147|

"When I entered this school, I just wanted to be a farmer after graduation. Now I know that I will further my study at the vocational college" (third-year male student, Su-won Agricultural Life Science High School).

"The students in Young-San Sung-Ji High are very different from those in ordinary schools. Girls wear earrings, high heels and make-up and have long hair."

STUDY SITES

Case study No. 1

Institutions:	**Su-won Agricultural Life Science (Senior) High School and Shingu Junior College**
Location:	**Kyong-gi Province, which includes 16 cities and counties just outside of Seoul**
Project starting date:	**1996**

A partnership arrangement between schools and junior colleges is offering vocational students a more interesting curriculum and giving them greater opportunities to go on to higher education.

Provincial contexts/overview

The "2 + 2" partnership between vocational high schools and junior colleges was introduced nation wide under the 1996 Education Reform Act. The first "2" stands for the second- and third-year in high school and the latter "2" represents the two years in junior college. The scheme is a response to the strong demands for higher education from vocational high school students and their parents. Partner high schools and junior colleges co-ordinate their curriculum and jointly develop textbooks. Partnership also entails sharing equipment and facilities, exchange of teaching staff and joint research activities. The scheme is expected to enhance vocational high school students' motivation significantly by providing a more interesting and co-ordinated curriculum and by boosting their higher education opportunities. Within Kyong-gi Province, where Su-won high school is located, 33 vocational high schools and 14 junior colleges are currently implementing this project and the number is increasing steadily.

Su-won high school has more than 1 000 students in four departments. Its plant resources department has linked up with two departments of Shingu College: Landscape Architecture and Horticulture. The main features of the Su-won-Shingu partnership are:

- *Admission procedure*: Up to 64 Plant Resources Department students are selected for the 2 + 2 scheme when they enter their second year. Half of them are eventually offered places at Shingu College without having to take an entrance exam (selection is based on criteria drawn up by the school). Sixteen of the selected students enter the Landscape Architecture department, while the remainder study Horticulture. The two departments reserve 20 per cent of their places for the Su-won students – the other 80 per cent are filled through open competition.

- *Curriculum reform*: The curriculum is jointly developed by Su-won and Shingu. Recognising that the existing curriculum is too theoretical, more practical elements, including some hands-on experience, have been introduced. This is expected to stimulate student interest and motivation for learning.

- *Textbook reform*: Joint textbook development has been in progress since 1998. A review of the existing textbooks revealed that the contents were too theoretical for high school students. Newly developed textbooks are tailored for students' comprehension level.

Starting with the 1999-2000 school year, the 2 + 2 scheme was integrated into the Ministry of Education's Autonomous Curriculum Project, for which Su-won was designated as a pilot school for three years. A "self-directed" learning cycle is the core concept for the project. The cycle begins with evaluation of one's own ability then it proceeds to preparation for learning, engaging in learning activities, and feedback, It finishes with a second evaluation of one's own ability. Some supplementary activities, such as work experience and problem solving, are also included.

Su-won's involvement in the Autonomous Curriculum Project will earn the school an additional 120 million won in provincial funding this year. This will pay for extra teaching staff and training, research in curriculum development and textbook design, as well as for facilities.

Outcomes

In 1999, exactly half of Su-won's 64 2 + 2 scheme graduates earned places at Shingu Junior College. Some of the remaining 32 went on to other higher education institutions. Overall, close to 60 per cent of Suwon's graduates entered higher education. This is considered as outstanding given the lower calibre of students in vocational high schools. Furthermore, the dropout rate at Su-won has declined from close to 13 per cent in 1995 to 11 per cent in 1998. The figure is considerably lower than the 20-50 per cent recorded in other vocational high schools in the province. Fewer behavioural problems were also reported by the school administration.

Students in the programme said that they were pleased to be given a clearer route into higher education. They also appreciated the positive personal accounts of "2 + 2" students who are now in Shingu Junior College. One high school student

149|

admitted that she had not excelled academically in her first year at the school, but she had studied hard to get into the "2 + 2" programme. And having being chosen gave her confidence to continue studying. Others said that they enjoyed the chance to gain more practical knowledge.

At Su-won, the 2 + 2 scheme is still in its formative stage. A co-ordinated curriculum is in place and textbooks are being produced, but so far the "2 + 2" practical classes have only been held during summer vacation and out of regular school hours. However, there is a plan to integrate the classes into the regular school day.

Although our schedule did not allow us to visit Shingu College, it was said that the recent expansion of higher education has resulted in junior colleges competing for students. Colleges such as Shingu are therefore eager to try this type of scheme.

Case study No. 2

Institution:	**Non-san Dae-gun Junior and Senior High School**
Location:	**South Choong-chung Province**
Starting date:	**mid-1980s**

South Choong-chung Province and one of its innovative church schools both recognise that students' personal development must receive as much attention as their academic progress.

Non-san Dae-gun Junior and Senior high is a private school for boys run by a Catholic organisation. The principal, who is a priest, strongly believes that all students, including low-achievers, should be given a proper education. Under his leadership, the teachers developed common goals in the mid-1980s. After a year of reflection, they started to implement new strategies.

The school's stated objective is "harmonisation of humanity education and high academic performance." This is put into effect through two main programmes focusing on personality development and high academic performance:

Personality development

Students build their own identity and develop a deeper understanding of human relationships through:

- *Extra-curricular activities*: Students are entitled to ask for any activity they are interested in and the school is committed to fulfil their request even if the interest is not shared by any other student. More than 60 activities are arranged and half of them take place outside of the school. Activities such as pottery, bakery and golf are run in collaboration with local residents or organisations.

- *Group and individual counselling*: Group counselling (12 in one group) is provided every Saturday. A trained counsellor is available but parents also volunteer for this work. The school believes that students tend to relate better to other children's parents and can talk through their problems and express their feelings. Students are most often troubled by relationship issues, especially those concerning friends. They rarely bring up other issues, such as violence or smoking. As low achievers tend to have relationship problems, assisting them in this way can also help their academic development.

High academic performance

Mobile classes: Students are grouped on the basis of their performance in specific subjects rather than their year groups. In the past, all classes would work at the same level in the same textbook. But now the pace of learning and course materials are adjusted to suit one's ability. Lower-ability students who might otherwise be inclined to give up if they encountered difficult work can now study the textbook tailored to their level and at their own pace. Peer support in learning is emphasised and all course materials were developed by the teachers themselves.

Two-hour classes: In order to shift from conventional one-way teaching to a learner-centred approach, two-hour classes replaced the conventional 50-minute classes. Under this new system teachers spend less time lecturing and provide more time for discussion or group activity.

Discussion and activity-oriented classes: These involve extensive use of hand-outs, which reduces the time that students spend copying information from the blackboard, and increases time for discussion. Korean language classes are discussion-centred and social sciences and sciences classes are activities-oriented, limiting the lecture time to 50-60 per cent.

Analytical capacity development: All subject studies are designed to be completed by the end of the second year of senior high. The third year is devoted to helping students develop their analytical powers.

Use of information and communications technology (ICT): The school uses the Internet in teaching and learning in a variety of ways. In science and geography, in particular, ICT is used extensively for classroom teaching.

Teacher training: This is provided every year. Teachers are also encouraged to take up numerous outside training opportunities. The school is about to introduce Stephen Covey's approach (1989) in its teacher training. It emphasises personal leadership and teaches people to teach themselves.

Funding: Government funding is said to represent about 60 per cent of school's total budget. Most of the rest comes from the standardised high school fees.

Both the provincial-level initiatives (see below) and the national reform of 1996 have provided an impetus to Non-san Dae-gun's long-standing programme. In the mid-1990s, the South Choong-chung provincial education office introduced a bold education system reform, called the "New viewpoint movement." The office prides itself on having been ahead of the national education reform of 1996. But it was the predominantly rural province's low ranking in a national exams table that was the immediate driving force for the change.

The movement is designed to prepare students for lifelong learning and the information age. Its goals are to:

1. Reduce the emphasis on memorising and cramming knowledge and see more attention paid to developing problem-solving and analytical skills.

2. Emphasise creativity, which is considered to be a key competency for lifelong learning.

3. Persuade schools to shift from a teacher-centred approach to a learner-centred one and develop self-directed learning.

The provincial governor, who is a published poet, said that the province had been actively researching ways of implementing these themes. He stressed that serious attention needed to be given to students' emotional development and maturity as well as their intellectual progress. The key characteristics to be developed include: entrepreneurial and optimistic attitude, concentration, and patience/self-control.

Outcomes

The province's reform efforts were rewarded in 1998 when it gained the top place in the national exam in which it had done poorly only two years earlier. As to Non-san Dae-gun high school itself, the principal stated that 90 per cent of its graduates go on to universities. He also said that other schools have started to implement similar innovations. At first, the Dae-gun parents were concerned that personality development was taking time out of subject learning but the school eventually convinced them that personality development had to come first if students were to excel academically.

Dae-gun's teachers exhibited a strong sense of ownership of their initiatives. This has been nurtured through the good working relationship with the school management. The school now has a complete set of course textbooks and a range of multimedia teaching materials, all of them made in-house. The teachers said they had devoted many hours of their own time to developing them. They had also helped one another to overcome some new technology problems and had concluded that ICT is a tool that needs to be carefully used. For instance,

tudents' concentration levels decreased considerably if they were asked to watch
a screen for a long time.

Case study No. 3

Institution:	**Young-San Sung-Ji High School**
Location:	**South Cholla Province**
Starting date:	**Mid-1980s**

**This liberal Buddhist institution is helping dropouts who were bitterly unhappy in main-
stream schools to discover that education can be enjoyable**

The drop-out rate in South Cholla Province is particularly low (1.2 per cent
in 1999). Yet its administrators see it as a significant problem. According to the
provincial education office, the low drop-out rate is mainly due to: i) An emphasis
on counselling; ii) The office's policy of encouraging schools to hold on to their
potential drop-outs and reduce the number of students being expelled for
breaching strict school regulations.

Only 10 schools in Korea are designated specifically for drop-outs. All of them
are running a distinctive, specialised curriculum. In South Cholla province, Young-
San Sung-Ji is the only school for drop-outs. It attracts students from all over the
country. The school has been specialising in this area since the mid-1980s when
rural-to-urban migration caused its enrolment to fall sharply. Prior to the mid-
1980s it was a normal high school. Between the mid-1980s and 1998, the school
was classified as a "special" school and it was outside the mainstream system.

Young-San Sung-Ji is a private school run by a Buddhist sect. It is located in
Young-kwang, a rural area about one-and-half-hours by car from Kwangju, the provincial capital. The school has 8 000 m^2 of land, of which almost half is farmed. It
also has a 180-bed dormitory but currently has only 83 students (21 girls and
62 boys). There are 18 staff members: principal, vice-principal, 13 teachers (including three part-time teachers), and three administrative staff. About 80 per cent of
the students came from broken families, and a third of them were in trouble with
the law before coming to the school.

Applications are accepted all the year-round and students are selected on the
basis of an interview and some scholastic and aptitude tests. The students pay
standard high school fees plus dormitory fees of 205 000 won per month. According to the school administration, the costs are not burdensome for most students'
families. However, after the economic downturn, some families are finding it hard
to pay the fees. The school is trying to help them by providing scholarships.

153|

The school's main goals are to develop students' personalities, appreciate individuals, encourage those who are willing to accept new challenges. It stresses the importance of social responsibility and moral education. When Young-San Sung-Ji was a "special school", it received no public funding. Since 1998, it has received some state money but has had to modify its curriculum to meet government regulations.

The school's liberal atmosphere, dormitory system and relatively small classes set it apart from most other Korean schools. Recognising that regular schools can be oppressive, Young-San Sung-Ji tries to make its students feel relaxed and comfortable. The students are consequently very different from those in ordinary schools. Girls wear earrings, high heels, make-up, and have long hair; boys wear baseball caps and some go barefoot. There are pool tables and pinball machines for teachers and students to play on together. Students are also allowed to play computer games when they do not have classes.

Students and teachers live in a "dormitory" like a family – nine students share three bedrooms and a teacher has the fourth. If the teachers have a family, they live near by. Every evening they have a group meeting to share their experiences. Additionally, each student has his/her own supervising teacher, so that they have access to counselling all the time. Teachers even volunteer to stay at school during holidays as some students cannot – or do not want to – go home because of their family circumstances.

Classes have fewer than 30 pupils (compared to 40 in regular schools) and the students are not divided by year groups. The educational experiences that are offered are also unusual. The Korean traditional music class, for example, emphasises group experience and practising rather than music theory. There are also special projects such as the organic hen farm and poultry factory that allow the students to be close to nature and to learn about self-sufficiency.

Students' liveliness during our visit was impressive. It was clear that they enjoyed their school life immensely. They said they could communicate with the teachers, who shared the chores with them and were unlike the authoritarian teachers in mainstream schools. The students liked the liberal atmosphere, which allows them to express themselves. They also appreciated the wide curriculum choice – physical education alone offers eight or nine options. One of the physical education teachers was a graduate from the school. He said that the time he spent at Young-San Sung-Ji in his teens was the most memorable of his life. He had been able to study at his own pace and had been given time to think about his future. As he believes his own experience makes him most suited to teach troubled students he had returned to the school after qualifying as a teacher.

)utcomes

As Young-San Sung-Ji has been quite successful the province is said to be con-
idering setting up more schools of this type. To date, 248 students have graduated
rom the school. A survey of their career paths that the school has conducted shows:
6 per cent went on to higher education, 21 per cent got a job, 11 per cent started
heir own business, 6 per cent entered public service, 9 per cent became monks, or
riests, and 17 per cent left to do military service, which is mandatory in Korea.

The school is, however, facing three major problems:

- *Pilot school status*: Under the current arrangement, the school has considerable control over its curriculum. However, there is some anxiety that the
  government may impose more control after 2001. At present, government
  funds cover teachers' salaries, equipment and facilities. The school supplements some operational costs by running profit-making businesses,
  including egg production.

- *Personality development programme*: By the time students come to the school,
  they are in many cases older than the normal high school age as there is
  often a time lapse between their dropping out and their re-entry into the
  system. As it is more difficult to change the behaviour of older students a
  three-year time frame is felt to be too short.

- *Need for earlier intervention*: At present, there are no junior high (middle)
  schools to cater for younger dropouts even though their number is growing.

Innovation and effectiveness

The goal of Korean education, "Education of Koreans as prospective leaders
for the 21st century" proved to be a strong, shared goal at all three levels of the
educational system (central, regional and school) and all regions visited during
the study. At the same time, decentralisation is a growing trend. Provincial education offices are adapting the goal and basing their policy priorities on their own
socio-economic realities. In all three study sites, provincial offices play a key role
in co-ordinating and supporting the initiatives. However, South Choong-chung
Province stands out because of its knowledge of current global trends and
research findings, and the fact that the provincial office and Non-san Dae-gun high
school mapped out their plans ahead of the central government reforms.

All three exemplars are combining several strategies to tackle student motiva tion: innovation in school curricula, new forms of teaching and learning, includin use of ICT, and innovation in partnerships. These approaches are on the sam lines as the system-wide educational reform and have shown some tangible out comes. The three study sites are not isolated examples; similar approaches ar being applied in other schools.

As echoed repeatedly by all concerned, one critical element in all the initia tives is the development of students' personality. Counselling and extra-curricula activities are placed in this broad policy perspective. This emphasis seems t come from a long-standing oriental ideology of looking at a whole human bein and integrating physical, spiritual and intellectual education. Recent concern fo adolescents' emotional development appears to have emerged from two inter twined insights: *i)* some reflection on the existing educational system's excessiv emphasis on subject-based competition and *ii)* a new understanding of the impor tance of the emotional side in relation to lifelong learning. The evidence pre sented in the study shows some notable achievements in this area. Howeve there should ideally be longitudinal research to gauge the long-term benefits.

Students liked new strategies which address what is missing in the existin educational system; flexibility, choice, outlets for self-expression, hands-on expe rience, and a tailored curriculum that provides increased higher education oppor tunities. Moreover, students' accounts suggest that a new teacher-studen relationship is developing. Gone are the days when someone in authority coul enjoy almost automatic recognition and respect. A new generation of student wants to be convinced that teachers and school administrators are worthy of thei respect. Only then can a new teacher-student relationship, based on genuin mutual respect and trust, be developed.

The teachers in the schools visited appeared to take the challenges ver well, seizing the opportunity to adapt their teaching and establish new relation with students. A sense of ownership among the teachers, coupled with a goo working relationship between teachers and school administrators, was certainly making a difference.

Public funding has just started to catch up with the government reform plans Private schools, which pioneered innovations well ahead of the government reform (Case studies 2 and 3), have to supplement their income by fundraising. As illus trated, public funding can help to legalise and formalise initiatives, but innovating schools are always conscious that it may reduce their autonomy and independence.

Transferability of strategies

Transferability of these initiatives should be quite possible within Korea a the cases presented are not isolated innovations (other examples under the same

r similar schemes are already in existence). The commitment and active involvement of both the central and provincial government will, however, be necessary. If
innovation is to spread and be sustained in other contexts, issues such as control,
accountability and funding will also be critical and need to be addressed in full.

Commentary

Korea is a populous country, which has experienced massive changes in an
unusually short period of time. With its relatively young population and rapid economic growth, just meeting the education needs of the people has been a tremen-
dous challenge at all levels of government. The pace of change also means that
the modern and traditional are currently coexisting side by side. The education
sector is not an exception. But the generational and attitudinal gaps seem particu-
arly wide in schools that are still characterised by excessive competition, strict
rules and authoritarian teaching.

The high societal expectations and parental investment mean that most
Korean students are strongly motivated to pursue higher levels of education.
However, the current economic downturn and increasing unemployment among
higher education graduates are calling into question the general assumption that
education leads to social mobility.

There have been bold and ambitious shifts in policy that take account of globalisation, technological revolution and lifelong learning. The government claims
that the planned reforms will fundamentally change the structure and operation of
the Korean educational system. It also points out that the next reform of 2002 will
introduce much more flexibility and freedom into the national curriculum. To what
extent it will impact on the system's core remains to be seen.

157

Bibliography

CHIN, S.H. (1995),
"The determinants and patterns of married women's labour force participation", *Korean Journal of Population and Development*, Vol. 24, No 1, July.

COVEY, S.R. (1989),
The 7 Habits of Highly Effective People, Simon and Schuster, New York.

KOREAN EDUCATION DEVELOPMENT INSTITUTE (1997),
An Analysis of Private Tutoring in Primary and Secondary School students, Seoul.

KOREAN STATISTICAL OFFICE (1997),
Korea's Social Indicators, Seoul.

LEE, M. (1997),
"Why do some women participate in the labour force while others stay at home", *Korean Journal of Population and Development*, Vol. 26, No 2, December.

MINISTRY OF EDUCATION (1998),
Statistical yearbook of Education, Republic of Korea, Seoul.

MINISTRY OF EDUCATION (1999),
Education in Korea 1998-1999, Republic of Korea, Seoul.

OECD (1998),
Education at a Glance – OECD Indicators, Paris.

OECD (1999),
Economic Outlook, Paris.

TIMSS INTERNATIONAL STUDY CENTER (1996),
Mathematics Achievement in the Middle School years, International Association for the Evaluation of Education Achievement (IEA), United States.

TIMSS INTERNATIONAL STUDY CENTER (1997),
Mathematics Achievement in the Primary School years, International Association for the Evaluation of Education Achievement (IEA), United States.

NORWAY

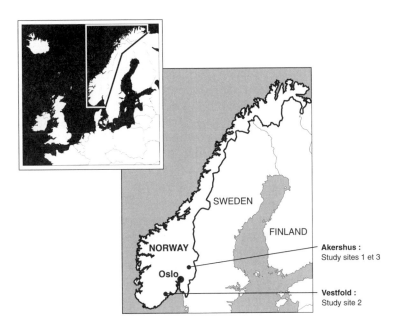

Land area in square kilometers: 324 000.

Total population (1998): 4 418 000.

Youth population – under 15 years (1998):
- 874 764,
- percentage of total population: 19.8%.

Youth unemployment (1998):
- 16-24 year-olds: 9.5%.

Percentage of 18-year-olds in education (1998): 88%.

Per capita GDP (1997 prices): 26 771 USD.

Birth rate per 1 000 population (1996): 13.9.

Sources: *Labour Force Statistics: 1979-1998*, OECD, Paris; *Annual National Accounts, Main Aggregates, Volume 1, 1999*, OECD, Paris; *Education at a Glance*, OECD Database 1999, Paris.

Country context

Education: The compulsory primary and lower secondary sectors are administered by 435 municipalities, while the 19 county municipalities are responsible for 535 upper secondary schools. Schools in Norway are generally small; there are, on average, fewer than 400 pupils per school in the compulsory sector and 330 in upper secondary schools. Students in the latter follow either general or vocational courses. The government and the Storting (the Norwegian parliament) determine the objectives of the education system and establish its framework. The Ministry of Education, Research and Church Affairs is responsible for administering the education system and for implementing national educational policy. Each of the 19 counties has a national education office carrying out central government functions. Nevertheless, considerable responsibility and decision-making powers relevant to education have been devolved from central to local government. Compulsory education is free, as are courses at publicly maintained upper secondary schools or training establishments. County authorities may, however, require students and apprentices to provide their own materials and equipment.

Economy: Norway is the least densely populated country in the OECD and its people are widely scattered. The country's demography therefore favours a decentralised structure of government. However, as a 1998 OECD study commented: "A traditional commitment to decentralised decision-making sits alongside, and at times uncomfortably with, an equally strong Norwegian egalitarian commitment to reducing geographical and social differences." The most important exports are petroleum, natural gas, foodstuffs including fish and fish products, paper and wood-related products and metals. Income from the North Sea oil industry is set to decline but the government has established a Petroleum Fund to accumulate financial assets and permit a smooth adjustment to the new circumstances. After several years of brisk growth there was a significant slowdown in the Norwegian economy in 1998, but the unemployment rate is still very low. In fact, a 1999 OECD economic survey of Norway reported: "The potential for expanding the labour supply was almost exhausted in 1998, with vacancies soaring and the unemployment rate dropping to below 3 per cent by the end of the year."

Student motivation issues

There are two contexts in which motivation of adolescents can be discussed in Norway. On the one hand, adolescence may be viewed as the intermediate stage between childhood and adulthood, a *rite de passage* that may lead to paid employment. On the other hand, adolescence can be seen as important for its own intrinsic characteristics, clearly encapsulated in the term "youth culture", in which the culture of upper secondary schooling is a part. The government seeks to provide appropriate curricula, pedagogy and institutional structures for different kinds of 16 to19-year-old students while seeking to create a foundation on which to build citizens for the future Norwegian economy and society.

This aim is expressed in the government publication (Royal Ministry of Education, Research and Church Affairs) outlining the core curriculum for primary, secondary and adult education:

> "Education shall qualify people for productive participation in today's labour force, and supply the basis for later shifts to occupations as yet not envisaged. It should develop the skills needed for specialised tasks and provide a general level of competence broad enough for re-specialisation later in life. Education must ensure both admission to present-day working life, and the versatility to meet the vicissitudes of life and the demands of an unknown future."

A very large proportion of 16 to 19-year-olds are in upper secondary education even though it is not compulsory in Norway. There is a statutory right to such education, and between 1980 and 1995 the proportion of 16-year-olds attending upper secondary schools rose from 72 to 95 per cent. In 1995, 83 per cent of 18-year-olds were enrolled in full-time education. Approximately 3 per cent drop out in the first 12 months of upper secondary education and, as in other countries, students following a vocational route are significantly less likely to complete their courses. Several factors help to explain this difference (Støren *et al.*, 1998):

- There are shortages of student places in particular kinds of vocational courses and a mismatch between the demand and supply of apprenticeship placements. There is evidence that women and immigrant students can suffer from discrimination if they apply for some popular courses and work placements.

- Students are generally dissatisfied with the existing curricula, with many feeling that there is insufficient emphasis on practical experience and too much on theoretical learning.

- Examination results from both lower secondary and the foundation level in upper secondary appear to have a significant impact on the completion rate, regardless of type and branch of study.

161

The appropriateness of the learning environment, including the design of school architecture and curriculum and examinations, must also be considered. As the background study produced for this report asserted:

"Lifelong learning is generally understood as learning which generates new learning, which is made possible because motivation takes the form of an inner driving force, rather than being the product of an external goal or ambition [...] students who have had their desire to learn mesmerised by previous experiences of failure in the educational system must establish faith in their own ability to learn, before they can learn how to learn."

The reform of upper secondary education appears to have made schooling for 16 to 19-year-olds more comprehensive and inclusive. For the students, school has become not just a place for academic learning but somewhere to grow up and become an adult. As the background study pointed out: the school becomes a place [...] to explore roles and to develop one's personal identity. It follows that if the school system is not able to accommodate the young people as a group, it is doubtful that it will ever be able to generate motivation for its prime objective, learning.

The challenge in Norway is seen in creating learning environments within schools that will motivate young people to continue to learn after they leave.

Main policy approaches

1994 marked a significant milestone in post-16 education in Norway. Reform 94 incorporated a number of changes intended to create a better co-ordinated system. All 16 to 19-year-olds on completion of lower secondary school or equivalent were given the right to three years of upper secondary education. They can now follow a route leading to vocational qualifications or a general pathway qualifying them for higher education. The right must normally be fully claimed within four years of completing lower secondary school and within five years when training is wholly or partly provided at a training establishment.

This merger of general and vocational training in one institution permitted the introduction of new combinations of courses and subjects. The first year is a foundation year. Three of the 13 courses available in this year prepare students for higher education while the other 10 lead to vocational qualifications. The basic structure for vocational training is two years of theoretical and practical training at school followed by two years of training and productive work in an enterprise. Specialisation takes place after the foundation year.

In addition to redesigning the curricula for the reformed upper secondary school the government drew up a core curriculum that extended from primary through to adult education. It was founded on the concept of the Integrated

Human Being who has six characteristics: spiritual, creative, working, liberally educated, social and environmentally aware. By studying these six human characteristics, it is argued, the student gains access to a variety of motivating experiences that the school as a learning organisation must provide. From the concept of the integrated Human Being can be derived core skills and competencies integrated in modules, subjects and courses that constitute the students' areas of study. This is thought to lead to motivation for lifelong learning.

The various study programmes list content and learning objectives but do not specify teaching methods. The ministry has, however, decreed that all upper secondary school students must engage in at least one cross-disciplinary project each year in which they apply the principles of active learning and extend them beyond the classroom. It is argued that this project work develops important skills, such as co-operation, creativity and analytical thinking and that successful projects give students a sense of achievement, providing them with tools for lifelong learning. Pedagogically, the project work is linked into the need for upper secondary schools to develop new roles for teachers and students, and give young people increasing responsibilities for a range of decisions and activities. The Storting anticipated that after Reform 94 was introduced students would help to choose the materials to be used, the teaching methods and forms of assessment. Experience so far shows that some schools are much closer than others to reaching those goals.

Reform 94 study programmes require the use of information and communications technology (ICT) and the government has emphasised the importance of ICT in promoting new ways of learning in its publication: ICT *in Norwegian Education – Plan for Action for* 1996-99.

Another key aspect of Reform 94 was the establishment of a follow-up service for school drop-outs. It is attempting to reintegrate early-leavers into school within the period of their statutory right so that they are able to gain an upper secondary qualification. This county-level service contacts all those who are entitled to an upper secondary place but fail to apply, as well as those who drop out of school. The assistance provided is closely tailored to individual needs.

Qualifications and certificates are regarded as ways of motivating young people to become lifelong learners. At the end of upper secondary education students can obtain vocational as well as academic qualifications needed for higher education. However, students are also entitled to individual, non-graded assessment. This is intended to motivate students for further, and possibly lifelong, learning through giving them continuous feedback on their work. This form of assessment was seen as a way for students to monitor their own progress without the possible demotivating factors of a graded scale. It also offers the potential for students and teachers, ideally as peers, to discuss the learning process in a broader perspective.

163|

A document – *The Guide* – published by the National Institute for Educational Resources in 1994 as part of Reform 94, encourages students to assume responsibility for their learning and urges them to take part in the school's democratic processes. The intention is to provide a tool for planning throughout the school year and support student-teacher dialogues. However, the overall objective of *The Guide* is to empower students by raising their awareness of the responsibilities and possibilities inherent in their role of active learners.

For vocational students, a Training Log has been introduced, listing learning targets and study programmes, and recording individual student progress. The log encourages a more systematic approach to training and raises apprentices' motivation by enabling them to monitor their own skills development.

The Education Act that came into force on August 1, 1999 gives students a statutory right to both counselling and education and career guidance. Over the past two years the National Education Offices have also received extra grants to support this area of work. The aim is to help students make well-founded education and career choices.

Teachers and education professionals also believe that students will be motivated by the new instruction methods that are being used to teach academic subjects such as mathematics and English within the vocational areas of study. The emphasis on theory has become stronger within these subjects but the teaching methods are also vocationally relevant. Reform 94 also supported the concept of entrepreneurship. The hope is that by focusing on this issue students will become more creative and innovative.

Since 1994, the period of compulsory education has been extended by one year to 10 years. In 1997, six-year-olds were required to attend school. Another significant piece of legislation, the Competence Reform, went through the Storting in May 1998. It stipulated that non-formal learning should be officially recognised as being of equivalent competence, even if it is not identical to what is laid down in study programmes and required for public examinations. In all subjects where it is practicable, adults have been given the right to sit examinations as external candidates and obtain the same qualifications as apprentices or students. Adults with approved vocational experience (five years of relevant work) who wish to document knowledge and skills acquired outside formal training may register for a craft or journeyman's examination.

The ministry has commissioned seven research institutes to evaluate Reform 94, and although motivation was not a principal issue, some of the research is of direct interest to this study.

From a goal document to classroom activity (Monsen, 1998)

This project evaluated the curriculum content of Reform 94 and looked at how the new learning environment was affecting motivation. It found that although some teachers remain skeptical about the reforms the experiences from project-based work have been more constructive than anticipated. A majority of teachers and students believe that the new curricula have made learning more profitable though the new common general subjects within the vocational studies branch have been heavily criticised. However, a majority of both teachers and students still believed that teachers should plan and implement teaching, and students receive it.

Locked up, shut out or included? (Kvalsund and Myklebust, 1998)

These two studies, which focused on young people with special needs, found that there was a wide range of factors undermining their motivation. The shift away from practical, co-operative experience in the workplace to more theory-based learning had not suited them.

Follow up or chased down? (Grøgard *et al.*, 1998)

Approximately 7 per cent of students with a statutory right to upper secondary education were in contact with the follow-up service during the 1998-99 academic year. This study found that few of those who work with this group believe it is possible to create an upper secondary school system able to accommodate all students. They would prefer to see more opportunities in the labour market and improved links between work and education.

"The core curriculum was founded on the concept of the Integrated Human Being who has six characteristics: spiritual, creative, working, liberally educated, social and environmentally aware."

"Kjelle school believes that students should be put in practical situations in which their freedom of choice is challenged."

165

Case study No. 1

Institution:	**Kjelle Upper Secondary School**
Location:	**Akershus**
Starting date:	**1995**

This renowned boarding school demonstrates that human beings really can change and develop even if they have experienced years of educational failure

Kjelle upper secondary school has built a reputation for adapting its teaching to suit students who are socially disadvantaged or have learning difficulties. It was therefore chosen to participate in a recent government-backed project that explored new ways of helping students who struggle to acquire vocational certification or qualifications that may give them access to higher education. Such students now have the right to gain partial qualifications and the Ministry of Education, Research and Church Affairs has been encouraging organisational, pedagogical and methodological strategies that will support this policy.

Kjelle school has a rural setting and is based in no fewer than 24 residential, administrative and teaching buildings scattered over a 100-hectare site that is approximately 80 km north-east of Oslo. The school's history can be traced back to the early 1940s when it catered for retarded boys and provided boarding facilities. Learning was originally tied to agricultural and shoemaking skills. Woodworking was introduced later. It was 1986 before girls were admitted and the range of subjects expanded. In 1993, the county municipality of Akershus took over the running of the school. Today, the school provides specially adapted learning in subjects such as Hotel and Food Processing, Woodworking, Building and Construction, Engineering and Mechanics, Health and Social Studies and in Management of Natural Resources. It also offers an ordinary foundation course in Management of Natural Resources and a supplementary year in forestry. Currently, there are 56 boarding students and 16 living outside the school.

All the Kjelle students have experienced previous educational failure. It is therefore crucial to motivate them towards, and establish faith in, the possibility of lifelong learning. The school tries to do this by applying three main strategies: the consequentialist pedagogical approach; the organisation of learning; and certification of non-formal learning.

The consequentialist pedagogical approach

At the heart of the school's curriculum is preparation for work. The principal emphasised that the school's goal was to develop the Integrated Human Being and quoted from the final paragraph in the government's Core Curriculum publication (Royal Ministry of Education, Research and Church Affairs). "The ultimate aims of education are to inspire individuals to realise their potential in ways that serve the common good; to nurture humanness in a society in development." To this he added the school's specific goals: "The students shall, after their education at Kjelle, have the qualifications to: get a job; keep a job; and be capable of coping for themselves on their own."

The consequentialist pedagogical approach is based on the belief that human beings, through their own choices, can change and develop. It is also a precondition that the leadership makes visible the basic values of the schools. The approach was adopted in order to prevent young people from dropping out of school and society. The school believes that students should be put in practical situations in which their freedom of choice is challenged and in which the various alternatives for action, and their consequences, are made obvious. The aim is to teach students to focus on future opportunities, rather than being stuck in past experiences. The approach also teaches students to be part of a community. The teacher's task is to make it clear to students that their actions have consequences that affect the community to which they belong.

If students are experiencing learning difficulties, teaching must be adapted and differentiated. This can be achieved through project-based learning and greater freedom of choice. At Kjelle, general studies are not timetabled and the students decide the content and duration of teaching. The latter may vary from 0 to 8 hours a week for each subject. Students are motivated by having to decide for themselves whether or not they need to gain competence in a particular subject.

Kjelle seeks to incorporate a company culture into the life of the school. It successfully combines vocational learning and production as witnessed in the woodwork area and in the horticultural nursery where the students sell their products. Learning is rooted in work experience and the social competence demanded by working life is developed by the execution of different tasks.

Certification of non-formal learning

Partial qualification has two main objectives. It should be regarded as a worthwhile goal in itself and it may also be used as a basis for engaging in further study or acquiring vocational competence. Individual curricula are worked out and learning is documented in personal reports. For those students who wish and are able to acquire complete competence it is crucial that learning, including learning adapted to meet special needs, is tied to the curricula within the different branches of study.

167

Only in this way may the education which students have already undertaken pay off. If the partial qualifications project succeeds in recognising and accrediting non-formal competence as well as the possibility of building on already acquired competence it will provide a stepping stone towards a job or further education.

Case study No. 2

Institution:	**Sandefjord Upper Secondary School**
Location:	**Vestfold**
Starting date:	**August, 1996**

Motivation levels will only flourish if schools are built on the right philosophical foundations – but this upper secondary school has found that the physical architecture can be important too

With 1 500 students and nine branches of study, Sandefjord Upper Secondary School is very large by Norwegian standards. It is located some 120 km south-west of Oslo and was established in its present form in 1996 when four schools in the town were integrated. The challenge has been to establish a unified school identity and to provide adapted learning for all students, regardless of circumstance. The school brings together general and vocational students, who are subject to the same administrative and organisational structure.

Senior staff emphasised that the school's prime objective is to create a community where students can exert real influence. From the outset it was realised that the new school would have a problem in dealing with such a large student body. This difficulty was aggravated by the design of the buildings, each having specialist, course-related functions. The need for a communal space was met by the construction of a building called the forum, a meeting place that includes a dining area, library, bookshop and what was described as a "base-camp of student services", including the follow-up service for school drop-outs referred to earlier in this chapter. The "base-camp" also has a health service, educational and careers service, and a teachers' workshop. The Forum asserts the importance of the school as a community.

It was argued that student motivation for lifelong learning rests on a foundation of responsibility and well being. To develop a learning environment in which these two elements flourish, the emphasis has been put on student participation.

There are traces of student participation in the curricula of the various branches of study, especially the learning tied to the production of saleable goods and the provision of services in the community. During the visit we were introduced to a simulated unit that manufactured soap from fish oil. The 12 students attending a vocational course were divided into three "shifts". Each had a shift leader and their work was focused on the manufacturing process, which was computer-controlled. As the process data were available on the Internet, students were able to work in collaboration with students in a German factory.

Student participation in the curriculum is at its most visible in the practically-adapted courses (*Praktiske Tilrettelagte Kurs* – PTK) which extend over five years, rather than the usual three. Students exert real influence over the individual curricula that are worked out to match their specific needs. One student was keen to describe a peer-education project that grew out of the International Baccalaureate scheme in the school. She explained how the students had taken the initiative by establishing groups in which young people could discuss issues relating to their personal well-being. Here we see students taking responsibility for important social issues, having the opportunity to develop problem-solving strategies and gaining new insights into their own and their peers' development.

Case study No. 3

Institution:	**Nesodden Upper Secondary School**
Location:	**Akershus**
Starting date:	**October 1998**

An ICT project at this school is demonstrating how new technology can smooth the path from traditional teaching to student-directed learning

Nesodden upper secondary school, which is less than 20 km from Oslo, has approximately 700 students and 90 teachers. It offers study branches in Health and Social Studies, Electrical Trades, Art and Design, General and Business Studies, and "APO" (Work, Production and Learning). The school is participating in a national ICT project that is exploring new ways of switching from conventional teaching to student-centred learning. The project is exploring the processes of change in: curriculum organisation, teaching methods and the use of technology to enhance learning.

Nesodden's ICT project involves students in three foundation course classes, of which one is a general subject class and two are vocational classes. It includes a variety of subjects such as Norwegian, English, Natural Sciences, IT, Economics and Sports and Physical Education. The county municipality has equipped the 55 students and 20 teachers with portable PCs that permit access to the school's website and the Internet.

An ICT unit at the University of Oslo is responsible for the in-service training of teachers and the preparation of students for the project as well as for its evaluation. The project's organisers hope that it will be applicable to other schools, educational institutions and learning environments where there are fewer computers.

The project is focusing on the learning process itself and its main objective is to highlight opportunities for developing new classroom strategies to promote learning. The possibilities for change and the motivational benefits found by merging new technology with new thinking about teaching methods are being explored. It is intended to incorporate ICT into the learning processes, rather than treat it as a separate subject.

Another important objective is to increase motivation through project work, problem-based learning and interdisciplinary activity, and it is recognised that ICT can help to achieve this. Problem-based learning presupposes that the students themselves collect, document and analyse the information they need to solve a problem. Furthermore, the ability to co-operate is acquired since students are dependent on each other to succeed in project work. The interdisciplinary approach promotes a greater understanding of relationships between various parts of the curriculum.

During the visit, two classes were observed using laptops, and opportunities were provided to discuss the project with students. In an art class, students were using a specially prepared workbook and associated software to learn about the use of colour in painting. In an English language class, individual students used Powerpoint presentations to demonstrate project findings. Data had been gathered from various sources, including the Internet, and the Powerpoint presentations included textual, visual and aural data. The students were enthusiastic about the ICT project and described many educational uses they had made of their laptops.

Although the project is still in its infancy, the University of Oslo researchers reported several preliminary findings:

- There has been a sharper focus on co-operative learning and problem-based learning.
- Teachers report that students seem more motivated towards their school work.
- Competence in using ICT has not been a problem for teachers, but the pedagogic changes are more difficult.
- Technical problems have not proved to be an obstacle.
- The learning environment has become more flexible and teaching approaches more varied in some classes.

Teachers reported that the students spend a lot more of their leisure time at school or at home solving problems. In addition, students have taken the initiative to organise computer courses for pensioners. For the future, teachers could see the potential of ICT-based teaching for those students requiring alternative curricula, home-based teaching, or other flexible learning arrangements.

* * *

Innovation and effectiveness

The projects described in this chapter must be viewed alongside the major educational reforms that have taken place in Norway in recent years. Reform 94 is at the heart of this. Not only did this reform introduce the statutory right for all students to receive upper secondary education, it also ushered in new curricula with supporting textbooks, examinations, in-service training, extended careers and guidance services and the follow-up service. The integration of vocational and general education was fundamental to the reform, as was the encouragement given to schools to develop new roles for students and teachers in curriculum implementation and in the establishment of partnerships with local communities. All of this was within a flexible framework founded on a concept of lifelong learning derived from a definition of the Integrated Human Being. The challenge for schools has been to match the idealism of the reforms to the practical realities of their local circumstances.

The integration of vocational and general education was obvious in the architecture of Sandefjord Upper Secondary where an attempt had been made to establish a community school that offered a wide range of curricular and extra-curricular opportunities. Modern and high quality accommodation was available for specialist teaching in many subjects, especially in music and sport. Students were encouraged to become increasingly confident and self-reliant by taking responsibility for environmental and enterprise links between the school and the community. There was an emphasis on student-centred learning and the need to give young people authentic experiences, well-illustrated by the school's link with a school in Soweto which has resulted in a student volunteering to work for an extended period there. Students appreciated this social, vocational and academic learning environment though they were critical of those teachers who continued to lecture and read from textbooks.

Teachers were critical of the rigidity of the school timetable but senior staff were trying to find ways to allow greater scope for more active and collaborative learning. It was also evident that there was still potential to develop the library as a learning centre. Furthermore, teachers needed to be seen more as mentors and less as instructors. The ICT project at Sandefjord was regarded as an important way of encouraging teachers of different subjects to work together to change teaching methods and modify student-teacher relationships. There was preliminary evidence from a formal evaluation project to indicate some positive changes.

Students and teachers spoke positively about the school as a community and the learning environments they encountered though no formal evaluation has been undertaken of the social and curricular progress that appears to have been made. The general view was that by making the school experience practical and relevant, in terms of the students' reality, motivation for lifelong learning was being promoted.

The importance of changing student-teacher relationships and redefining the role of the teacher was highlighted in Nesodden school. While the introduction of laptops for teachers and students was interesting in itself, it was the use of the laptops to trigger alternative styles of teaching that was more significant. This concern with pedagogical reform to match the structural changes brought in by Reform 94 ran as a thread through the discussions with teachers and students in the three schools visited. The ICT project was shared with other schools and the effectiveness of the innovation cannot be judged at this early stage.

Matching the statutory right with the curriculum framework poses a challenge, especially when students may have general or specific learning difficulties, social and/or emotional problems. The partial competence arrangements are designed for these students. A survey conducted in 1996 in Akershus and Oslo showed that of 225 companies in 21 sectors nearly 80 per cent needed employees with partial qualifications. The matching of vocational education to companies' needs is an important challenge and is embedded in the Norwegian goals for lifelong learning. The evaluation project identified strengths and weaknesses in the provision. However, the visit to Kjelle illustrated how a shared sense of purpose in a specially designed learning environment – a rural boarding school – can motivate students and teachers. Students spoke positively about both the curriculum and pedagogy and were responsive to the principles and practice inherent in the consequentialist approach. The effectiveness of the Kjelle programme was judged by the employability of the students and their capacity to be self-reliant in educational and social contexts.

Transferability

Projects in each of the three schools visited were shared with other schools in Norway. Thus the ICT project was envisaged as a pilot project with specified goals and it was being externally evaluated. The strategy of using new technologies to motivate young people to take more responsibility for their own learning has to be seen alongside the use of ICT for altering teaching methods and establishing new student-teacher relationships. There is rich potential for sharing the experience that teachers have gained through the ICT projects. Given the integration of vocational and general education in the upper secondary school, there may be opportunities within the pilot schools for teachers in various subjects to benefit but also there is likely to be transferring back and forth across the vocational-general divide. The findings of the pilot projects could also be disseminated more widely through in-service education and publication of the evaluation reports.

The importance of dissemination was emphasised by the Kjelle staff who reported that more than 1 000 Norwegian teachers had visited the school in the previous year. While the boarding element is a unique aspect of the school, the three key features of its learning environment – the consequentialist approach, the organisation of learning, and the certification of non-formal learning – have direct relevance for other upper secondary schools.

The importance that Sandefjord school invests in its architecture – for achieving pedagogical and social educational goals – also merits wider consideration. While it is easy to identify the use of the Forum as a flexible, communal space providing a range of commercial and student support services it is more difficult to assess the way in which conventional classrooms are being adapted to meet changing methods of teaching. It would appear that such changes can be introduced more easily into the more flexible arrangements of workshops and laboratories than into general studies classrooms.

Commentary

The substantial and comprehensive changes for which Norway has legislated have brought about structural and organisational innovations in upper secondary education. Evaluation studies show that schools have embraced the pedagogical and social implications of these reforms in a variety of ways. Students express criticisms of old-fashioned teaching methods and assert the importance of course content that is realistic and authentic. Some teachers, aware of these criticisms, refer to the inadequacies of in-service training that emphasises administrative and bureaucratic aspects of the reforms at the expense of active learning, co-operative learning and the use of the new technologies. Researchers and teachers point out that parents' traditional images of secondary education can make it difficult to bring about pedagogical changes.

What this points to is the need for thorough dissemination strategies to be implemented over a period of time following legislative change. Several teachers suggested that the government vision needs to be fully understood by teachers and students as well as by administrators. In the words of a student leader: "There needs to be an investment in people as partners." Teachers need incentives to introduce change and these do not have to be financial. Administrative demands may inhibit pedagogical change, as will inflexible classroom design and furnishings.

Nevertheless, Norway has established a coherent and well-planned system for achieving lifelong learning and there is evidence in evaluation reports and from the school visits that students have more opportunities to exercise responsibility and acquire self-reliance, independence and confidence. In the words of the background report for this study:

"Schools with an *active view* of students emphasise that they bring with them resources to build on, rather than shortcomings to overcome. The aim is to give students the experience of being valued on the basis of their own capabilities and skills. By relating to young people in this way the school will also treat them as equals. Within this framework it is much easier to develop a climate marked by confidence and trust, which are important preconditions for motivation and learning."

Bibliography

GRØGARD, J.B., MIDTSUNDSTAD, T. and EGGE, M. (1998),
  Følge opp eller forfølge? (Followed Up or Chased Down?), Fafo, Oslo.

KVALSUND, R. and MYKLEBUST, J.O. (1998),
  Innestegning, utestegning eller inkludering? (Locked up, Shut out or Included?), Volda, Møreforskning.

MONSEN, L. (1998),
  "From a goal document to classroom activity", Forskningsrapport 42/1998, Hoegskolen i Lillehammer, Lillehammer.

NATIONAL INSTITUTE FOR EDUCATIONAL RESOURCES (1994),
  The Guide, Oslo.

OECD (1998),
  "Thematic Review of the Transition from Initial Education to Working Life. Country Note: Norway", March.

OECD (1999),
  Economic Surveys Norway, p. 9, Paris.

ROYAL MINISTRY OF EDUCATION, RESEARCH AND CHURCH AFFAIRS (undated),
  Core Curriculum for Primacy, Secondary and Adult Education in Norway, Oslo.

STØREN, L.A., SKJERSLIE, S. and AAMODT, P.O. (1998),
  I *mål* (Reaching the Finishing Line?), NIFU, Oslo.

UNITED KINGDOM

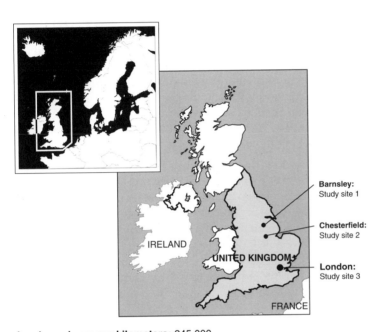

Barnsley: Study site 1

Chesterfield: Study site 2

London: Study site 3

Land area in square kilometers: 245 000.

Total population (1998): 59 237 000.

Youth population – under 15 years (1998):
- 11 373 504,
- percentage of total population: 19.2%.

Youth unemployment (1998):
- 16-24 year-olds: 12.3%.

Percentage of 18-year-olds in education (1998): 49%.

Per capita GDP (1997 prices): 20 483 USD.

Birth rate per 1 000 population (1996): 13.0.

Note: Data above are for the United Kingdom but this report relates only to England.
Sources: *Labour Force Statistics: 1979-1998.* OECD, Paris; *Annual National Accounts, Main Aggregates, Volume 1, 1999,* OECD, Paris; *Education at a Glance,* OECD Database 1999, Paris.

Country context

Education: While educational attainment has risen sharply since the early 1980s, the overall level is still low in comparison with several other developed nations, particularly in maths, and many young people still leave school without basic skills or qualifications. The Labour government is determined to improve education standards and a number of policy documents issued by the Department for Education and Employment over the past three years have underlined this commitment. A national curriculum was introduced in the late 1980s by the previous conservative administration and nationally-normed tests in core subjects are administered at the ages of 7, 11 and 14. The results of these tests are publicly available and the 11-year-olds' scores are published by national newspapers in the form of school league tables. In addition, schools are subject to regular appraisals by the government's inspection body, the Office for Standards in Education, and its reports are also publicly available. There is a high level of accountability in the English system with an emphasis on quantitative data.

Economy: The United Kingdom economy is experiencing a sharp slow-down, following a six-year expansion that saw unemployment decline to its lowest level in two decades. In 1998, just over 6 per cent of the labour force was out of work – but the jobless rate began to edge up again at the beginning of last year. The number of people employed in manufacturing has shrunk, while many new jobs have been created in the service sector. There is, however, a mismatch between the skills that employers require and those that the unemployed have to offer. Although this is a universal phenomenon it may be a particular problem in the UK as 7 000 000 adults in Britain, *i.e.* more than one in five, have poor literacy and numeracy skills. The UK was consequently placed ninth out of 12 industrial countries that took part in the recent OECD/Statistics Canada International Adult Literacy Survey. Although the UK is a member of the European Union, it chose not to join the European Economic and Monetary Union in 1999.

Student motivation issues

Although many people in England achieve high levels of competence and qualifications through school and post-compulsory education there is still a deep learning divide (Fryer, 1997). As in some other OECD countries, economic development in England has gone hand in hand with the widening of social and economic inequality. There is evidence of disaffection, alienation and hostility to education among many teenagers, and there continues to be considerable inequality of access to further and higher education. While 80 per cent of 18-year-olds from senior managerial and professional backgrounds enter higher education, only 10 per cent from unskilled backgrounds do so. As elsewhere, initiatives that were designed to increase participation have inadvertently contributed to, rather than alleviated, social and educational exclusion.

Only a quarter of English adults describe themselves as current learners and one in three has taken no part in education or training since leaving school. A recent labour force survey found that only 14 per cent of all employees had been receiving job-related training and the National Advisory Council for Education and Training has pointed out that one third of employees have never been offered any kind of training by their employer. Ten per cent of 16-year-olds are neither in education nor the labour market and over 40 per cent of 18-year-olds are not currently in any kind of training or education.

The background paper prepared for this study by Dr. Derrick Armstrong of the University of Sheffield provides a valuable review of the UK literature on student motivation and alienation. He quotes a 1982 study by Hargreaves (Hargreaves, 1982) which argues that if schools do not give their pupils a sense of belonging, or the feeling of being valued as contributing members of a cohesive social group, they will turn elsewhere to meet this basic human need. The result will then be seen in disaffected adolescent groups in which members draw strength from their opposition to the schools' norms and culture.

Armstrong refers to several studies that emphasise the importance of whole-school approaches to the problem of disaffection and lack of motivation. He questions the effectiveness of programmes in which children are withdrawn from the classroom for special teaching and points out that these programmes can create a sense of helplessness in class teachers. In such cases, the child has been assessed as requiring special help, which by definition they are not qualified to provide. On the other hand, offering class or subject teachers support in their work with pupils with learning or behavioural difficulties can give them confidence and a sense of control. In principle, he suggests that this can also send positive messages to pupils by implying their ability to cope with the mainstream curriculum.

He cites evidence from a British study, which shows that pupils with low non-verbal reasoning scores were more likely to be demotivated than pupils with higher scores (Galloway *et al.*, 1998). However, as he adds, the findings of other UK researchers suggest that variations in the effectiveness of schools, on a range of dimensions, cannot be explained wholly by differences in pupil intake. They also show how pupils' rate of progress can be affected by individual teachers or by subject departments in a secondary school. These differences tend to be larger than those between schools. Many of these studies implicitly raise questions about the extent to which the examination system and competition between and within schools affect student motivation.

It is worth bearing this in mind when evaluating education initiatives, the success of which is measured by examination or test results. Norm-referenced testing inevitably ensures that there will be some relative successes and failures. The link between failure, or perceived failure, and motivation, particularly in the context of lifelong learning, should not be overlooked.

Nevertheless, it is important that young people be set intellectually challenging tasks and goals. As Armstrong says, if there is no challenge there is nothing to master. Yet, intellectually challenging teaching carries the risk of failure for the pupil. It is also risky for teachers who may lose control of their class and face complaints from colleagues and parents.

It can be argued that the British school system's preoccupation with outcomes and normative comparisons makes it difficult for pupils who are unlikely to achieve high grades to become strongly motivated. However, we know that some schools and some staff in every school do provide intellectually challenging teaching to which pupils of all abilities respond positively. Moreover, in some of the schools visited in connection with this study we can see that student achievement appears to have improved in spite of, or perhaps because of, the competitive system.

The anti-work peer culture that students encounter in many schools is another powerful demotivator. But this is not merely a problem for secondary schools. One comparative study of the attitudes of French and English primary children found that many of the English children did not want to be best in the class. They were also "lukewarm about getting a good mark or even praise for good work. Some children actually said they did not want to be seen as too good by the teacher; no French child said this" (Osborn, 1997).

One further point should be made when discussing motivation in English education. Recent studies have highlighted the fact that boys are doing less well than girls in various tests, particularly in reading. In general, boys appear to be less motivated than girls, particularly in their early teens. This is an issue that is causing widespread concern and further studies will have to be carried out to identify the underlying causes. But research into girls' educational problems is needed too. "Wasted Youth", a recent study by the Institute for Public Policy Research, reported that they are just as likely to become truants and not be in training, education or work at the age of 17.

Main policy approaches

The revised Strategic Framework to the year 2002 of the Department for Education and Employment, *Learning and Working Together for the Future*, states that the government wants Britain to become a society that is (Department for Education and Employment, 1999):

- *Inclusive*: giving everyone the chance to fulfil their potential and in particular offering a future to those who are disadvantaged.

- *Prosperous*: where individuals continuously develop the skills they need to remain employable and help businesses to be competitive.

To achieve these objectives, the government has adopted a policy programme that is underpinned by six overlapping themes:

- *Raising standards and attainments*: seeking providers to raise the achievements of pupils, students and trainees in schools, colleges and training.

- *Encouraging innovation, diversity and new ways of working*: looking for fresh solutions to problems and being prepared to operate in different ways to achieve lasting results.

- *Promoting inclusion and equality of opportunity*: working to overcome the barriers that exclude individuals and groups from learning and sustained employment.

- *Increasing access and participation*: making learning much more accessible and encouraging a much wider proportion of the population to become learners.

- *Enhancing employability and skills*: promoting learning that enables individuals to develop skills that will help them secure and retain jobs in the future.

- *Developing a community focus*: supporting the efforts of local communities to manage their own regeneration.

The government is providing additional resources to achieve these objectives. It has launched a number of initiatives that seek to improve participation rates in education and training post-16, make learning in schools more desirable and attractive, and motivate adolescents to commit themselves to lifelong learning. What follows is a selection of initiatives to illustrate the scope of relevant government reforms in England.

In 1996 a major review of qualifications for 16 to 19-year-olds (*The Dearing Report*, 1996) made recommendations for changes in the three principal pathways for this age group: academic, applied (vocationally orientated for full-time students) and vocational (for school-leavers). The changes were intended to motivate young people to stay in education and training. Under recent government proposals all students will have new National Records of Achievement.

181

Unemployed school-leavers at 16 include the most socially disadvantaged young people and special arrangements have been made for them. For two years they have access to new National Traineeships. Older unemployed (18-25 years) are registered under the New Deal introduced by the government in 1998 and they may undertake work for environmental organisations or undergo either full-time or part-time education and training. For the employed there are Modern Apprenticeships, to which National Trainees can progress. Schools and colleges are encouraged to make work experience available for all 16 to 19-year-olds. In November 1998, the government launched new partnership projects for disaffected 14 to 17-year-olds. These projects bring together schools and local organisations in work-related activities, as illustrated in the Thirty-Nine Steps Initiative (see Case study 2 below).

The partnership concept has been further developed by the Education Action Zones initiative launched by the government in 1998. Partnerships of local education authorities, parents, businesses and Training and Enterprise Councils have been invited to bid for funds for innovative projects that will yield higher levels of achievement and increase students' motivation levels. Projects can include specialist schools (for example, in the arts, languages or technology), literacy summer schools, family learning schemes and work-related learning. The first 12 zones started work in September 1998 with a further 13 in January 1999.

An Action Plan for the Inner Cities was launched in 1999, emphasising the importance of developing the aptitudes and abilities of all students, not least the very able and talented. It is argued that "An inner-city location does not justify low standards and aspirations among teachers, pupils or parents".

The government is paying much attention to ICT and several new technology initiatives intended to modernise teaching methods should make learning in schools and colleges more attractive and motivating. They include: the Superhighway (providing on-line interactive databases, video-conferencing and access to learning resources) and the National Grid for Learning (a network of resources centres including public libraries, local education authorities and schools and colleges).

"Only a quarter of English adults describe themselves as current learners and one in three has taken no part in education or training since leaving school."

"The training for curriculum support assistants has had a demonstrable impact on pupil motivation and achievement."

Case study No. 1

Project:	**Training programme for special needs assistants (SNAPT)**
Location:	**Barnsley, south Yorkshire**
Starting date:	1997

The motivation and attainment levels of children with special educational needs have improved thanks to an innovative training programme for teaching support staff

This programme is administered by the local education authority in Barnsley, a large industrial town in the north of England. The local economy has suffered from the collapse of the coal-mining industry and unemployment is high. Barnsley is also handicapped by a low skills base because of the previous reliance on traditional industries. Attainment levels in the town are far lower than the English average and there are much higher levels of identified special educational needs, disaffection and absenteeism.

Barnsley tries to offer places in mainstream schools – rather than special schools – to children who have been assessed as having special educational needs. Following psychological assessment, a statement of the special support and facilities that will be required by these children to benefit optimally from school is provided. Hence, the phrase "statemented pupils" is sometimes used to describe these children. In general, they are assigned adult support in the form of a special needs assistant or a curriculum support assistant (CSA), who works with them in the classroom. A training programme for CSAs provides the focus for this case study. The SNAPT programme was designed not only to provide specialised training for these assistants but ultimately to improve the motivation and achievement of the pupils with whom they worked. The programme started in January 1997. It was developed by Sue Baskind, an educational psychologist with Barnsley Education Authority, as part of her doctoral studies.

The programme aims to:

- Provide assistants with the skills and knowledge necessary to work more effectively with pupils who have learning and/or behavioural difficulties.
- Enable assistants to work more effectively with teachers who have pupils who are experiencing such difficulties.
- Provide a nationally-recognised accreditation programme of training for classroom assistants.
- Encourage assistants to enhance their general level of education and identify and pursue specialised areas of professional interest.

183

The project has had a demonstrable impact on pupil motivation and achievement arising from the training. It illustrates how measures aimed at raising the self-esteem of adults can help children from the same community.

Kirk Balk Secondary, a comprehensive school with about 1 000 pupils, is one of the schools involved in the training programme. The percentage of pupils with statements of special needs is twice the national average (5 per cent compared with 2.4 per cent). There are 15 CSAs in Kirk Balk and it was clear from talking to the assistants, the teachers and the school management, that the training programme had had wide-ranging benefits. The reading and comprehension ages of the children who were supported by the CSAs who had taken the SNAPT course had been appreciably enhanced in comparison with pupils whose assistants had not received the training. The trained CSAs were operating at a higher level than one would normally expect from such staff. For example, individual CSAs had specialised in particular areas of the curriculum and, in collaboration with the subject teachers, had prepared differentiated programmes for the children under their care.

In one of the lessons that was observed, a CSA was assisting four pupils, and her responsiveness and understanding of their needs was impressive. In another class a group of pupils with very low communication and intellectual skills gave a presentation that suggested they had a healthy degree of self-esteem and motivation. The social and interpersonal skills of these pupils appear to have been enhanced by the work they are doing, and the CSAs have played an important part in their development. The usual performance indicators, such as GCSE results (GCSE is the examination that English pupils take at 16), would have been inappropriate for these pupils. However, they had worked towards the Award Scheme Development and Accreditation Network (ASDAN) award and were proud of the certificates and achievements in their portfolios. They clearly had an understanding of the tasks they had undertaken and demonstrated a palpable sense of involvement and commitment.

Case study No. 2

Project:	**The Thirty-Nine Steps Initiative**
Location:	**Chesterfield, Derbyshire**
Starting date:	**September 1998**

A work-experience project has enabled a group of local employers to establish an unusually close bond with teenagers who have little or no interest inconventional schooling

This project is run by Derbyshire Education Authority, North Derbyshire Training and Enterprise Council and Derbyshire Chamber of Commerce. It is one of 21 action-research projects that the Department for Education and Employment

1as funded. The projects are spread across England, from Devon in the Southwest 1o York in the Northeast, but the common aim is to provide a work-related programme 1or 14 to 16-year-olds that will improve their motivation and achievement. These 1rojects are currently being evaluated to assess whether they are transferable to a 1arger number of pupils.

The Thirty-Nine Steps initiative is a two-year programme for 20 disaffected 1upils. In the first year, they spend 39 days with staff at the Chamber of Commerce, 1nd in the second, a further two days a week with employers.

The project has been conceived as a five-stage developmental process. The 1model is designed to improve pupils' motivation and attitude by developing spe-1ific basic skills, building personal confidence and commitment, and raising 1wareness, knowledge and understanding of the world of work through direct 1xperience.

The other key objectives are to:

- Provide each 13-year-old with an additional careers interview and detailed plan (discussed and agreed with pupil and parents) which safeguards the pupil's entitlement to breadth, balance, equality of opportunity and progression from the ages of 14 to 19.

- Offer a comprehensive programme of induction and preparation tailored to meet each pupil's needs and identify for each pupil a named mentor in the work-place.

- Create opportunities to strengthen basic skills and develop the key skills of application of number, communication and information technology.

- Ensure that in-school and out-of-school curriculum experiences complement each other.

- See that out-of-school programmes contribute to accredited qualifications.

- Monitor each pupil's attendance, progress and achievements and provide them with feed-back each term.

- Identify the research, processes and activities that contribute to raising individual pupil achievement.

Ten pupils have been selected from each of two local secondary schools to par-ticipate in the project. We met seven of these pupils – from Parkside Community School in Chesterfield – and discussed the project with them. While they appeared to be quite alienated from school and from society, they clearly enjoy being involved in the project. They have developed an exceptionally good relationship with the project co-ordinators in the Chamber of Commerce who have provided a great deal of support for individual pupils. The project emphasises the develop-ment of personal and social skills, and courses on drug-awareness, smoking, sex education, and team-building are among its most important elements. In addition,

185|

skills in lifting and handling, health and safety, and fire safety are developed, and ultimately certificated.

However, one might question the extent to which the project is integrated into their schooling experience. They are withdrawn for one day a week from their normal lessons and this causes some discontinuity. These concerns have been identified by the two evaluators from Sheffield University and will no doubt be addressed. As is often the case, the project's apparent success owes a lot to the exceptional dedication and commitment of the staff involved who take a personal interest in each of the participants and provide support and counselling. It is too early to tell whether the project has helped to raise achievement levels. But even if it has not, other indicators should be considered: for example, a greater willingness to communicate with adults, the development of independence and self-esteem, and the ability to take relevant decisions and to act responsibly.

The close relationship between these young people and the staff of the Chamber of Commerce was certainly impressive. The role of the chamber in supporting training initiatives seemed to be atypical of chambers of commerce generally, but was praiseworthy and relevant. The chamber employs a number of full-time staff and operates from a fine building in Chesterfield that has its own training workshops and a cafeteria where the food is prepared by catering students. It also organises off-site training courses, and because of its close links with local employers, the chamber is particularly well placed to arrange work-placements.

Other pupils in the school consequently envied the 10 who had been chosen for the project and many pupils have expressed an interest in participating next year. One wonders, however, whether work placements that involve the Chamber of Commerce might not be offered to every pupil in schools such as this. The removal of a few pupils for one-fifth of the school programme without making any arrangements to compensate them for these lost lessons is a matter of some concern and is likely to be reflected in their academic results. It might also be useful if the staff of the school we visited were more integrally involved with the project. Closer links between Chamber of Commerce representatives and school staff, particularly those involved in personal, social and health education and counseling programmes, could also pay dividends.

Case study No. 3

Institution:	**The Edgware School**
Location:	**London borough of Barnet**
Starting date:	**1997**

The new head of a school that appeared to be sliding towards disaster has set challenging goals for students and staff. His efforts seem to be having the desired effects

The Edgware School is situated in Barnet, a north London borough that is economically and ethnically diverse. Barnet has a school-age population of 47 500 and operates a mixture of selective and comprehensive schools. The Edgware School draws its pupils from neighbourhoods that are characterised by high levels of unemployment, poverty, poor housing and social deprivation. The school is an 11 to 18, co-educational and multi-cultural secondary. It is non-selective and at the time of the OECD visit had 1 014 pupils on roll. Almost half of them (46 per cent) are designated as having special educational needs, and the same percentage are from poorer families who are entitled to free school meals. Just over a third of pupils (35 per cent) have English as a second language and they speak no fewer than 51 languages at home. In 1997, attendance levels had fallen below 85 per cent. The proportion of students gaining five or more higher-grade GCSEs (the national examination taken by 16-year-olds) had declined from 33 per cent in 1994 to 14 per cent in 1997. The school was at the bottom of the borough league table for examination results and was the ninth worst secondary in the country in tables comparing improvement/decline between 1994 and 1997.

In September 1997, a new head teacher was appointed and immediately introduced a strategy of improvement and change. These changes took place within the policy context of the UK government's White Paper, *Excellence for Schools,* and also within the borough's corporate plan for 1998-2002. This committed the borough to improving standards in education for all its children.

The school's new strategy involved:

- *Setting expectations for staff, students and parents.* Clear targets were drawn up for subject areas and new thinking encouraged.
- *Symbolic improvement.* This included changing the name of the school, implementing a GBP 120 000 redecoration and refurbishment programme and rewriting the school brochure.
- *Vision.* The head teacher gave pupils and staff a clear and realistic vision of what the future could hold and how it could be achieved.
- *Evidence collection.* Barnet Education Authority was asked to review the school's curriculum, attendance and finances. The evidence gathered

187|

formed the basis of school-development planning. Evidence on pupil progress was also systematically collected and deployed.

- *Line management*. Structures were established with clear responsibilities.
- *Self-review*. A policy of self-review for students and teachers was introduced in partnership with the local authority.
- *Coalition for change*. The head teacher set about creating a group of those involved in the school – teachers, parents and governors – who were prepared to push change forward.
- *Target-setting*. A programme of interviews and mentoring was established for all year 10 and 11 students.

The head teacher invited Dr. Elizabeth Leo from the Institute of Education, University of London, to assist at some of the sessions with students at which expectations were raised and goals were set. The head teacher was already familiar with the literature on school improvement and is currently reading for a doctoral degree at the Institute of Education.

Outcomes to date

Between 1997 and 1999, a number of identifiable improvements occurred. By the end of the first year:

- The proportion of pupils gaining five or more good GCSEs (A* to C) had improved from 14 per cent to 28 per cent.
- Attendance levels had risen from 80 per cent to 91 per cent.
- Literacy standards in year 7 (11 and 12-year-olds) had improved by 50 per cent.
- The average points totals gained by A-level exam candidates (18-year-olds) had increased by more than 50 per cent.

Interviews with students, particularly higher-achieving 18-year-olds, indicated that they appreciated the new challenges that were set for them. They said that teachers now had higher expectations of them, and that they worked harder to achieve these goals. They spoke positively about the individual interviews and review meetings that they had been offered. They suggested that their self-esteem had increased as a result of these exercises and that this was reflected in their GCSE results. Attendance rates have improved and exclusion rates have fallen. In 1995-96, 135 students were excluded either permanently or temporarily for breaching school rules, and this rose to 163 in 1996-97. In 1997-98 that number fell to 70 and it was expected to drop to below 60 during 1998-99.

Some of the teachers also appeared to be excited and motivated by the new approach and spoke positively about the changes. However, the new approach resulted in a large exodus of staff, some of them long-serving teachers, at the end of the 1997-98 school year. About 20 of the 60 full-time-equivalent teachers chose to leave and the school has had to search hard to ensure that quality replacements were found. It is impossible to judge whether the entire teaching staff have bought into the new culture of school improvement but they are co-operating with the measures taken.

The head teacher's overall achievement in only two years is impressive. It will be interesting to see whether this improvement can be sustained during the coming years.

* * *

Innovation and effectiveness

Each of the projects visited is effective in its own way. Each has strengths and areas where further development might occur. It is also interesting that universities provided back-up for each of the projects. These initiatives had been carefully planned and developed; their goals were clearly defined and the results were being rigorously evaluated.

Given the national emphasis on product and outcomes in education, it is not surprising that each project emphasised academic achievement. It might be argued that this received too much attention. However, it is notoriously difficult to measure motivation and it will be many years before anyone can say whether these projects improve attitudes to learning or encourage their participants to engage in lifelong learning. Even so, there is some preliminary evidence that the self-esteem of the young people involved has been raised. Their behaviour also seems to be more positive and they appear more co-operative. They understand the importance of working with their peers in a constructive and non-aggressive way. The use of portfolio assessment with the special needs pupils in Barnsley and the accumulation of certification in areas such as health and safety and first aid in Derbyshire are examples of how demotivated young people can sometimes respond to continuous and formative assessment that provides more immediate recognition of success.

In all three projects there was considerable emphasis on the pupil as an individual. In Derbyshire, the emphasis on individual counselling by Chamber of Commerce staff had encouraged pupils to stay with the programme and had apparently raised their self-esteem and motivation levels.

All three projects were characterised by exceptional commitment and involvement of staff. In fact, the project leaders may find it hard to sustain their current workloads. Some questions might therefore be raised about the long-term sustainability and generalisability of these approaches, although much of the workload may become routine after the initial set-up period.

The academic goals of the projects are another concern. Where pupils' academic performance is being measured, it should be compared with their own previous performance and not always against those of their peers or a national average. The staff involved in these projects are well aware of these distinctions but sometimes appear to be pressured by national requirements. It would be a pity if the apparent successes of these projects, in terms of personal and social development, were unrecognised simply because academic performance indicators showed little improvement – not that this is likely to be the case.

Bibliography

DEARING REPORT (1996),
> "Review of Qualifications for 16-18 year Olds", March.

DEPARTMENT FOR EDUCATION and EMPLOYMENT (1999),
> *Learning and Working Together for the Future – A Strategic Framework to 2002.*

FRYER, R.H. (1997),
> *Learning for the Twenty First Century: First Report of the National Advisory Group for Continuing Education and Lifelong Learning,* November.

GALLOWAY, D., ROGERS, C. and LEO, E. (1998),
> *Motivating the Difficult to Teach,* Longman, London.

HARGREAVES, D.H. (1982),
> *The Challenge of the Comprehensive School: Culture, Curriculum and the Community,* Routledge and Paul Kegan, London.

OSBORN, M. (1997),
> "Children's experience of schooling in England and France: some lessons from a comparative study", *Education Review,* Vol. 11 (1).

Main References

Part One

GAGE, N.L. and BERLINER, D. (1979),
Educational Psychology, Rand McNally.

GARDNER, H. (1993),
Multiple Intelligences: The Theory in Practice, Basic Books.

OGISU-KAMIYA, M. (1997),
"HRD (Human Resources Development) in a Multicultural Workplace: The Need For Lifelong Learning", in Hatton, M.J. (ed.), Lifelong Learning Policies, Practices & Programs, School of Media Studies at Humber College (APEC Publication #97-HR-01.5), Toronto, Canada.

OECD (1995),
Our Children at Risk, Paris.

OECD (1996),
Lifelong Learning for All, Paris.

OECD (1997),
Literacy Skills for the Knowledge Society: Further Results from the International Adult Literacy Survey, Paris.

OECD (1998a)
Education at a Glance – OECD Indicators, Paris.

OECD (1998b),
Overcoming Failure at School, Paris.

OECD (1999a),
Labour Force Statistics: 1979-1998, Paris.

OECD (1999b),
National Accounts, Vol. 1, 1960/1997: Main Aggregates, 1999 Edition, Paris.

OECD (1999c),
"Thematic review of the transition from initial education to working life – Country Note: Norway, Finland, UK", Paris.

THE JAPANESE MINISTRY OF EDUCATION, SCIENCE, SPORTS AND CULTURE (Monbusho) (1998),
Statistical Abstract of Education, Science, Sports and Culture, 1998 edition.

TIMSS INTERNATIONAL STUDY CENTER (1996),
   Mathematics Achievement in the Middle School years, International Association for the Evaluation of Education Achievement (IEA), United States.

TIMSS INTERNATIONAL STUDY CENTER (1997),
   Mathematics Achievement in the Primary School years, International Association for the Evaluation of Education Achievement (IEA), United States.

Part Two: Country Case Studies

Denmark

ANDREASEN, L. *et al.* (1997),
   Unge uden uddannelse (Young people without education), AKF Forlaget, Copenhagen.

ANDREASEN, L. *et al.* (1998),
   Veje til forbedring og fornyelse af ungdoms-uddannelserne? (Way to Improve and Renew Youth Education), AKF, Copenhagen.

CHRISTENSEN, F. (1999),
   The Important and Innovative Features of the REFORM-2000 of the Danish VET System, Ministry of Education, Copenhagen.

DANMARKS ERHVERVSPÆ-DAGOGISKE LÆRERUDDANNELSE OG UNDERVISNINGS MINISTERIET, ERHVERVSSKOLEAFDE-LINGEN (1997),
   Egu i praksis – erhvervsgrunduddannelse (Basic Vocational Training – Egu in practice – examples of good practice), Copenhagen.

OECD (1995),
   Reviews of National Policies for Education – Denmark: Educating Youth, Paris.

OECD (1999),
   "Thematic review of the transition from initial education to working life – Country note Denmark", Paris.

SKOV, P. (1998),
   Unges fremtid – meget afgøres tidligt – erfaringer fra en forløbsundersøgelse (The future of young people – much is determined early – Experiences from a progress survey), Danmarks Pædagogiske Institut, Copenhagen.

TAMU (1998),
   The Training School – Labour Market Training for Youth – Basis, Documentation, Development Træningsskolens ArbejdsMarkedsUddannelse, September.

UNDERVISNINGSMINISTERIET (1995),
   Vejledning om brobygningsforløb til ungdomsuddannelse (Guide to bridgebuilding courses to youth education).

Finland

KOMITEANMIETINTÖ (1996),
   Elinikäinen oppiminen tietoyhteiskunnassa: II *osamietintö*, Koulutussuunnittelun neuvottelukunnan mietintö (Lifelong Learning in an Information Society: II Partial report: Strategic Choices, Report of the Advisory Committee on Educational Planning), October.

KOMITEAMIETINTÖ (1997),
    The Joy of Learning: A National Strategy for Lifelong Learning, Summary of the Report of the Lifelong Learning Committee appointed by the Finnish Government.

HAVÉN, H. (1999),
    Education in Finland 1999: Statistics and Indicators, Tilastokeskus, University Press, Helsinki.

OPETUSMINISTERIÖN (1997a),
    Näkökulmia elinikäiseen oppimiseen, Elinikäisen oppimisen komitean mietinnön Vol. 14, liiteosa, 2, painos, Oy Edita Ab, Helsinki.

OPETUSMINISTERIÖN (1997b),
    Terveen itsetunnon ja elämänhallinnan edistäminen peruskoulussa, Opetusministeriön työryhmien muistioita, Vol. 29.

SINKO, M. and LEHTINEN, E. (1998),
    Bitit ja pedagogiikka. Tieto-ja viestintätekniikka opetuksessa ja oppimisessa. Osaamisen uudet haasteet ja tietotekniikan mahdollisuudet, Sitran julkaisusarja nro 194, Atena Kustannus (The Challenges of ICT), WSOY, Jyväskylä.

Iceland

BERNBURG, J. and THORLINDSSON, T. (1997),
    "Ofbeldi, lifstill, samfelag: thaettir tengdir ofbeldi, afbrotum og vimuefnaneyslu medal unglinga" (Violence, Life Style, Society: Elements Connected to Violence, Crime and Drug Abuse Among Teenagers), U*ppeldi og menntun – Timarit* KHI (The KHI Magazine: Upbringing and Education), Vol. 6, pp. 65-78.

BILDDAL, S. (1993),
    "Hugmyndir nemenda um nam og störf" (Pupils' Ideas on Studies and Work), Paper for Education and Culture, University of Iceland.

GUDMUNDSDOTTIR, G. (1998),
    Fjölmenntabraut Borgarholtsskola – Skyrsla um throunarstarf (Borgarholt Comprehensive School – A Report on Developmental Work), Report written for the Ministry of Education, Reykjavik.

JONASSON, J. and JONSDOTTIR, G. (1992),
    Namsferill i framhaldsskola – Helstu nidurstödur (Study Progress in the Secondary School – Main Results), Report for the Ministry of Education, Social Science Research Institute, University of Iceland, Reykjavik.

KARLSSON, T., SIGURDARDOTTIR, G. and THORLINDSSON, T. (1993),
    "Skrop nemenda i framhaldsskolum og tengsl thess vid adra thaetti i skola, lifsstil og andlega lidan" (Truency Among pupils in Secondary Schools in Relation to Other Elements in the School, Life Style and Mental Health), Upp *eldi og menntun – Timarit* KHI (The KHI Magazine: Upbringing and Education), Vol. 2., pp. 62-85.

MINISTRY OF EDUCATION (1998),
    Enn betri skoli – theirra rettur okkar skylda (A Far Better School – Their Rights – Our Duties), Reykjavik.

OSKARSDOTTTIR, G. (1995),
    The Forgotten Half: Comparison of Dropouts and Graduates in Their Early Work Experience – The Icelandic Case, Social Science Institute, University of Iceland, Reykjavik.

SIGURDARDOTTIR, G. 1991),
"Göfgar vinna med nami? Nidurstödur rannsoknar a thattum tengdum vetrarvinn⬚ framhaldsskolanema" (Is Working with School Sublime? Results From a Research o⬚ Elements Related to Winter Work Among pupils in Secondary Schools), *Rannsoknarrit 1* Research Institute for Education and Culture.

Ireland

DEPARTMENT OF EDUCATION AND SCIENCE (1998),
Adult Education in an Era of Lifelong Learning – Green Paper on Adult Education, Governmen⬚ Publications, Dublin.

DEPARTMENT OF EDUCATION AND SCIENCE (1998),
Schools IT 2000; A Policy Framework for the New Millennium, Government Publications Dublin.

GARDNER, H. (1993),
Frames of Mind (2nd edition), Fontana Press, London.

GOVERNMENT OF IRELAND (1997),
Sharing in Progress, National Anti-Poverty Strategy, Dublin.

HANNAN, D. *et al.* (1996),
Coeducation and Gender Equality, Economic and Social Research Institute, Dublin.

HANNAN, D. and SHORTALL, S. (1991),
The Quality of Their Education, Economic and Social Research Institute, Dublin.

KELLEGHAN, T., MADAUS, G. and RAZCEK, A. (1996),
The Use of External Examinations to Improve student Motivation, American Education Research Association.

NATIONAL ECONOMIC AND SOCIAL FORUM (1997),
Early School Leavers and Youth Unemployment, Forum Report No. 11, Dublin, January.

STOKES, D. and WATTERS, E. (1997),
Ireland: Vocational Education and Training – A Guide, Leonardo da Vinci, Dublin.

SMYTH, E. (1999),
Do Schools Differ?, Economic and Social Research Institute, Dublin.

Japan

AMANO, I. (1984),
The Challenge to "The Learning Society", Nihon Keizai Shimbunsha, Tokyo.

ITIKAWA, S. (1985),
The Theory and Structure of Lifelong Education, Kyoiku Kaihatsu Kenkyujo, Tokyo.

ITIKAWA, S. and USHIOGI (1979),
The Education Course 21: The Road to the Learning Society, Gakken, Tokyo.

KAGAWA and MIYASAKA (1994),
Creation of Lifelong Learning, Mineruva Shobo, Kyoto.

MORI, MIMIZUKA and FUJII (1986),
"The Door to Lifelong Learning?" *Idea, Theory and Measures,* Gyosei, Tokyo.

OKAMATO, K. (1994),
Lifelong Learning Movement in Japan? Strategy, Practices and Challenges, Tokyo.

SATOU, K. (1998),
   Lifelong Learning and Social Participation, University of Tokyo Press, Tokyo.

SAWANO, Y. (1997),
   "Lifelong learning: An instrument for improving school education in Japan?" in M. Hatton (ed.), *Lifelong Learning: Policies, Practices and Programs*, APEC Publication, Toronto.

Korea

BAE, S. (1998),
   "Measures to use internal motivation", *Education Research*, Vol. 18, No. 9.

CHO, Y. (1997),
   "Students' motivation and lively class atmosphere", *Education Research*, Vol. 17, No. 4.

CHUNG, H. (1996),
   "The effect of jigsaw co-operative learning on self-image, Internal motivation and academic performance", Master's Thesis at Choong-ang University.

CHUNG, H. (1998),
   "Students' motivation through Feedback", *Education Research*, Vol. 18, No. 9.

CHUNG, M. (1997),
   "Middle school students' motivation and co-operative learning", *Education Research*, Vol. 17, No. 5.

EDUCATION COMMISSION (1995),
   Education Reform Measures for New Education Systems.

EDUCATION COMMISSION (1996),
   Education Reform Measures for New Education Systems.

LEE, D. (1998),
   "Students' motivation under the open education", *Education Research*, Vol. 18, No. 1.

LEE, N. (1997),
   "Individual Learning and Motivation", *Education Research*, Vol. 17, No. 1.

MINISTRY OF EDUCATION (1997a),
   Reform Bill on Curriculum for Primary and Secondary Education.

MINISTRY OF EDUCATION (1997b),
   Comprehensive Measures for Education and Welfare.

MINISTRY OF EDUCATION (1998),
   Education Statistics yearbook.

YANG, M. (1998),
   "Students' Motivation through Using Learners' Questions", *Education Research*, Vol 18, No. 9.

YOO, I. (1998),
   "Measures to Promote Attentiveness for students' Motivation", *Education Research*, Vol. 18, No. 9.

Norway

GRØGARD, J., MIDTSUNDSTAD, T. and EGGE, M. (1998)
   Følge opp eller forfølge? (Followed Up or Chased Down?), Fafo, Oslo.

KVALSUND, R. and MYKLEBUST, J. (1998),
Innestegning, utestegning eller inkludering? (Locked up, Shut out or Included?), Volda: Møreforskning.

MONSEN, L. (1998),
"From a goal document to classroom activity", Forskningsrapport 42/1998, Hoegskolen Lillehammer, Lillehammer.

ROYAL MINISTRY OF EDUCATION, RESEARCH AND CHURCH AFFAIRS (1997),
The Transition from Initial Education to Working Life, Oslo.

ROYAL MINISTRY OF EDUCATION, RESEARCH AND CHURCH AFFAIRS (1998),
The Competence Reform in Norway, Report 42 presented to the Storting (Norwegian National Assembly), May 28.

ROYAL MINISTRY OF EDUCATION, RESEARCH AND CHURCH AFFAIRS (undated),
Core Curriculum for Primary, Secondary and Adult Education in Norway, Oslo.

SKÅRBEVIK, K. and BÅTEVIK, F. (1998),
Kompetanse for alle? (Competence for All?), Volda, Møreforkning.

STØREN, L., SKJERSLIE, S. and AAMODT, P. (1998),
I mål? (Reaching the Finishing Line?), NIFU, Oslo.

United Kingdom

BLUMENFELD, P. (1992),
"Classroom learning and Motivation: Clarifying and expanding motivational theory", *Journal of Educational Psychology*, Vol. 84, pp. 272-281.

DEPARTMENT FOR EDUCATION AND EMPLOYMENT (1998),
Excellence in Schools, London.

FRYER, R. (1997),
"Learning for the twenty-first century. First report of the National Advisory Group on Continuing Education and Lifelong Learning", Department for Education and Employment, London.

GALLOWAY, D., ROGERS, C., ARMSTRONG, D. and LEO, E. (1998),
Motivating the Difficult to Teach, Longman, London.

KENNEDY, H. (1997),
How to Widen Participation: A Guide to Good Practice, Further Education Funding Council, London.

OECD PUBLICATIONS, 2, rue André-Pascal, 75775 PARIS CEDEX 16
PRINTED IN FRANCE
(96 2000 03 1 P) ISBN 92-64-17193-2 – No. 51089 2000